Clinetta –

Body Bag Religion

GREG WILLIAMS

May God Bless You on this "adventure"!

Greg Williams

John 10:10

authorHOUSE®

AuthorHouse™
1663 Liberty Drive, Suite 200
Bloomington, IN 47403
www.authorhouse.com
Phone: 1-800-839-8640

First published by AuthorHouse 6/10/2008

ISBN: 978-1-4343-9023-3 (sc)
ISBN: 978-1-4343-9024-0 (hc)

Printed in the United States of America
Bloomington, Indiana

This book is printed on acid-free paper.

I DEDICATE THIS BOOK:

To Lisa, the very heartbeat of my life.
Thanks for always believing in me and encouraging me to go beyond what I think I can do myself. Not only are you the love of my life and my soul mate, but you are my very best friend. I would not be who I am if it wasn't for your never ending love and compassion that you share with me each and every day. All my dreams have been fulfilled in having you as my partner through this adventure called life. I look forward to spending the rest of our lives together. Thanks for being EXACTLY who you are! I love you with all my heart.

To Uncle Ray and Aunt Dorothy, my guides during my childhood. As I look back on my early years, both of you have made a life changing impact on my upbringing. You were always there for me and the Christian values that I hold so dearly today are from your guidance and instruction. When I enter into heaven I hope you are the first couple I see after I spend a few moments in the presence of my Creator. I miss you each day of my life.

To Mom, the pillar of my life.
You always believe in me. You always support me. You are always there. I couldn't ask for a better mom. I thank God everyday that you are the mother that He chose just for me.

To Burny Burnett, the encourager.
Lisa and I's life has been so blessed since you have entered into it. We have discovered in our journey through this life that real lifelong friends are so hard to find, but we have truly found one of the best in you. Thanks for your love, kindness, encouragement and laughter. You always seem to bring a ray of sunlight into our daily lives. Thanks, buddy.

To the special family of friends (and you know who you are). Thanks for allowing me the freedom to be myself without the fear of being judged by you. I appreciate your willingness to accept me with all my flaws and faults and you still choose to love me. I will never take that lightly and for the rest of my life I will forever be grateful. It is an honor to be your pastor, but most of all it is even a greater honor to call you my friends!

Saving the best for last, to my Lord AND Savior, Jesus Christ. The gift of life couldn't be experienced without the life that You gave for me at Calvary. Thanks for loving me enough to die on the cross and for saving this filthy sinner. I can't wait to be in Your presence and look into Your eyes and my hope and prayer is that I can bring a smile to Your face.

Contents

Acknowledgements

As I sit in my recliner typing this book on my laptop computer, I glance over at my wife, Lisa and smile. There are just people that God puts in your life that makes you smile. Think about it. You have those people in your life, too. Think, glance and smile. Go ahead. Your face won't break. I promise. Then I look at the pictures that are hanging on the walls of our home of the kids. Then I smile again. Ashton, Matt, Kelan, Blake and Curtis. Five smiles in a row.

But wait there's more. The girls. Lexi and Maci. The little bundles of joy that most people call dogs, but not in our home, they are the girls. I can't help but smile again.

I think that's what this book is all about. Remembering those things that make you smile and acknowledging them before it's too late. Taking the chance to live life to its fullest and not being afraid to enjoy it.

I want to "tip my hat" to so many people. I know better than try to name them individually, but to those that have supported my ministry and my calling over the years, I thank you. I really am blessed to have your love and friendship. By the time this book is published I will have spent 25 years of my life preaching the Gospel of Jesus Christ. What? 25 years? Don't believe me? I have the gray hairs and the "crow's feet" to prove it. Have I made mistakes? Oh, yeah. Do I have regrets? Far too many. Do I wish I could change a few and make some of the past disappear? No doubt. But failure only can become failure when you decide not to get up when you fall down. That's life!

I would like to take this opportunity to acknowledge a few of my professional ministry mentors that I have respected over the years:

*Charles Swindoll. Chuck, when I read the book "Living Above the Level of Mediocrity", my entire life was changed. Thanks for allowing God to use you and your pen.

*John Hagee. John, your powerful messages have encouraged me for years to "keep on keeping on." Thanks.

*Paul Crouch. Paul, your vision and drive to reach the world for Christ has always been a blessing to me. You may not know it now, but I will be on your TBN program and have the opportunity to sign a song to the entire world. Another dream on my list.

*David Jeremiah. David, your most recent book, "Signs of Life" was the encouragement that I needed to complete this book that Christ had placed in my heart. It was a "Turning Point" in my life.

I would like to conclude this acknowledge section with a special, last but not least, mention to some special individuals. To all those believers that I have had the privilege to lead to Christ throughout all my years of ministry, I thank you. Every time I have had the honor to share the "sinner's prayer" with a new believer it has brought deeper meaning to my life. I will never forget you and my prayer is that you may always remember that day that your life became ALIVE through Jesus Christ.

If you haven't had the opportunity to ask Jesus in your heart, don't put this book down until you read the Epilogue at the end of this book. It will change your life forever.

Before You Begin

"One of the greatest tragedies in life would be, to wake up one morning dead and discover that you had never lived."
-Greg Williams

You may be wondering as you pick up this book, "What's the big idea with this book?" "What is this crazy preacher trying to accomplish by spending several months of his life writing these 21 chapters?" Well, please allow me a few minutes to explain the purpose, message and goal of this book. Ready? Let's go.

I have always been fascinated with death. The concept, the science, and the emotion of physical death have been an interest to me since I was a child. I can vividly remember each and every death that occurred in my life over the past 45 years. One thing that I am very thankful for is that my parents never tried to shelter me from death by not allowing me to be involved or trying to prevent me from grieving in my own special way. Because of this freedom, I feel that I have a great attitude and understanding of the meaning of death.

But that's not exactly what this book is about. It's about death, not just physical death, but something far greater and much more tragic… spiritual death. It amazes me that over the twenty five years of pastoral church work, the amount of death I have witnessed. Once again, not physical death, but spiritual.

I feel that one of the great tragedies of a Christian life is to never have experience true living. Can that be possible? Absolutely! Just show up at your own church this Sunday morning and watch. Listen to the singing. Look into the eyes of the members. Do you see life? Do you see passion and purpose and excitement and enthusiasm? I'm afraid that in probably more than 90% of the churches in the United States, you'll experience the very same thing. Death.

My intent of this book is to compare the characteristics of physical death to the characteristics of spiritual death. The book is divided in three sections: Section One deals with the condition of the individual Christian and an in depth look at the apathy and lack of life that is being experienced. Section Two opens the door into the church and the casket, corpse and condition it is in. Section Three has been written to help bring life back into each person that reads this book and applies the principles of life that is outlined in God's Word.

Please notice that the book is designed to read only one chapter per day for the next 21 days. 21 days? Is there significance here? Yep. Leading professionals have discovered that it takes exactly 21 days to create habits and/or break bad habits. That's my prayer for you. Spend the next 21 days to develop a life-changing routine. Make an effort for this routine to include spending quality time with Christ and creating a life plan for your purpose and destiny. Don't rush through this book. Take it a chapter a day. Write your thoughts. Journal your feelings. Pray your wants and wishes to the Master. Allow this process to change your life.

Three weeks. On the 7th, 14th and 21st days you will notice that there has been included a day of Reflection and Review. Don't just skip over this. Spend some time rereading a few chapters and making sure that you are catching all the concepts. Underline. Circle. Highlight. Make this book your tool along with your Bible. A tool for life.

At the beginning of each chapter is a famous quote regarding life and death. At the end of each chapter you will find two small sections called, "Written in Stone" and "Final Words." "Final Words" will feature an infamous phrase uttered with from final breath of a famous person. "Written in Stone" will give you a glimpse at a notable epitaph on a gravestone somewhere in the world. I told you I was fascinated with death. I thought these extras would be interesting and entertaining while we take this journey together.

If something touches your heart and you would like to share it, please e-mail me at bodybagreligion@yahoo.com. I would love to hear from you and I will try my best to respond to each and every e-mail.

Now take a deep breath. Turn off the TV. Find your favorite "quiet" place and fasten your seat belt. You are about to take an adventure into the world of death. Take a good look while you are there. Don't forget what it looks like. Don't forget what it smells life. Don't forget what it feels like. Remember, today is the day that you start to climb out of the coffin, jump out of the grave and really live. Are you ready for life?

CHAPTER 1
A Trip To The Morgue

"Life and death are balanced on the edge of a razor."
-Homer in Iliad

The day starts like so many days before. You slap the snooze button three times in the last 20 minutes hoping that it will reset the clock so that you can sleep for a few more hours before facing the day. But this day is different. Similar to so many before but different.

After your mind slowly awakens trying to convince your body to do the same, you remember that the dawn has broken through the darkness. Not the physical darkness that had covered the rural small town that you reside in, but the emotional darkness that won't be lifted until you face the event of the day that you have dreaded for past several turns of your daily planner.

A trip. Not just an ordinary trip. A journey. Not just an ordinary journey.

The freshly brewed coffee only alerts your senses that reality will soon be revealed. A quick shower, shave and brushing of your teeth only prepares you for the external effects of the event. Nothing can prepare you for the internal conflict. Your stomach starts to churn as you check the expiration date on your coffee creamer. Finally realizing that the java additive hasn't caused the nausea, the anticipation of the journey has.

With a big sigh, you grab your car keys and begin the trip. The trip you've dreaded can no longer be avoided. As you back out of the driveway, you begin to create excuses why you shouldn't go but there isn't enough creativity in you to stop the trip. You turn on the radio trying to take your mind off the day but the gloomy news broadcast only adds another layer of despair.

So the silence in the car seems to scream louder and louder as you finally arrive at the destination you have so dreaded. You notice that other cars are in the parking lot realizing that you may not be alone as you had hoped. Sometimes days like this can be endured better alone. Alone to think through your actions. Alone to filter your emotions and plan your next move.

As you enter the building, a blast of coldness strikes you hard in the face and more noticeably in the gut. The frigidness doesn't come from the large air conditioning units. The cold wave is the lack of emotion in the air. Everything seems so....so.....DEAD.

A member of the staff directs you to the room and shows you where to sit and wait for the inevitable. Your stomach starts to churn and knot up again. It's just a matter of time now. As you glance at your watch you are reminded of the despair by the lulling of funeral music in the air. "Where do they get this stuff?" "Is there a company that actually produces this somber and depressing music?" It makes elevator music seem like a polkafest.

The time has come. The clock strikes reminding you that there is no way out. It's here. The moment has arrived.

A tall, thin emotionless man enters to your left and makes his way to the front of the room. As he does, you wipe the sweat off of your brow anticipating and dreading the aftermath. You take a deep breath and wait. The director clears his throat and prepares to begin event that you have tried to avoid all morning. He says, in a zombie-like tone, "Please get your hymnals and turn to page 335 as we begin our morning worship service."

The dreaded event wasn't a trip to the morgue where actual dead bodies are collected and displayed. The journey was a journey to a place where hundreds of thousands of people arrive each week. A place called church. Sadly, there are so many similarities between a morgue and church that is makes your head spin.

This book will take you on a detailed adventure through what I call, "Body Bag Religion". I will reveal to you how death has entered into churches and auditoriums all across our nation and the prescription to bring the "body" back to life.

Take time to read only one chapter a day. They are short enough to maybe even read over twice to get the complete picture and then meditate, pray and think through the contents along with the scriptures.

Now is the time to take action. Reach up and grab the zipper on your personal body bag and start to break out of the cycle of death and come back to life. Now! Before it's too late.

CHAPTER 2
I See Dead People

Dead: 1) deprived of life: no longer alive
2) having the appearance of death:
lacking power to move, feel or respond

"I see dead people. They don't know they're dead. They're everywhere." A famous quote from a great movie, "The Sixth Sense". This phrase can be so easily applied to the individual Christian life. People walking around pretending to be alive, but in reality they are experiencing death in the fullness.

You know who they are. They stand out like a sore thumb. Dead. They just don't know it. They have a laminated church membership card in their wallet or purse. They don't miss Sunday morning worship service. They look the part, or should I say, "act" the part. But they are dead.

This first section of the book will deal with the individual Christian that has died inside but hasn't let their brains and hearts know it yet. Their spouse knows it, their children know it, even everyone at the office knows it. Dead.

I look around me, and I see a lot of people who are not experiencing their life at all. There is no joy in the ride. They are just not enjoying life very much; they are just enduring it. There are people around us who are simply marking time, counting off days and months as if they were prisoners in a cell placing another mark on the wall for another day that has just past. How unfortunate!

Jesus Christ tells us in John 10:10, *"I've come that you might have life and live it to the fullest."* Do you have any idea what that verse is telling us?

1. There really is a Full Life."

It does exist. And Christians all around us have discovered what it is and how to live it. And so can you!

People who enjoy life to its fullest will possess all of these qualities: love, joy, peace, patience, kindness, goodness, faithfulness, gentleness, self-control, compassion, purity, humility, modesty, faith, character, wisdom, enthusiasm, dignity, optimism, confidence, honesty, and a relationship with God. In other words, the abundant life is full of all the things money can't buy. No matter how much money you have, you can't buy more patience, self-control, or salvation! Hardware stores do not sell wisdom or hope. And yes, you can possess all of these qualities! You can get everyone of these things from God, who is the giver of all good things. The Bible says, *"Every good and perfect gift is from above, coming down from the Father of the heavenly lights, who does not change..."*, James 1:17. But the Bible also says, *"You do not have, because you do not ask God,"* James 4:2.

Are you in pursuit of the abundant life?

2. The "Full Life" is free from the things that are bad for us.

Everyone who wants to experience the full life should try to avoid the following negative qualities: Selfishness, hatred, lust, unforgiveness, envy, jealousy, fear, drunkenness, sexual immorality, discord, fits of rage, dishonesty, greed, gossiping, slander, pessimism and despair. In other words, people with these issues often spend lots of money on Prozac, therapy and marriage counseling in order to keep it from destroying themselves and their relationships.

The more these negative qualities are a part of a person's behavior, the farther they are from obtaining this thing called the "full life" or "abundant life". And yes, God can remove all of these negative characteristics from a person's life. Every one of them! God is greater than our sins! At one time, the people of Corinth, lived a life full of much wickedness and evil, but when Jesus was introduced to these people, by the power and grace of God, many were able to free themselves from these immoral actions. Paul wrote in 1 Corinthians 6:11 *"And this is what some of you were. But you were washed, you were sanctified, you were justified in the name of the Lord Jesus Christ and by the Spirit of our God."* If the Corinthians were able to get free from these destructive behaviors, by the grace of God, this means that you can, too.

It doesn't matter that you are hot-tempered, for example. God can change that in you! So it's no longer an excuse to say, "This is who I am and I can't change that. You must accept me as I am!" No, we don't. People who are living the abundant life don't walk around like a warm can of soda-pop that is about to explode at any minute. Everybody can be free from their personal weaknesses causing pain and embarrassment to themselves. That's just one of the benefits of living the full life.

3. The 'Full Life' is found in Christ and nowhere else.

Everyone who does not have Jesus in their life will not be able to experience the true and full life. No doubt, many non-Christians can experience some happiness and satisfaction in their lives, but that is usually because they practice the qualities that make up the abundant life, such as patience, integrity, and kindness. They also avoid many of the things that destroy the abundant life such as despair, pessimism, sexual immorality, substance abuse, etc. However, Jesus said that unless we believe in Him, we will all die in our sins, John 8:24. We must, therefore, realize that no matter how much happiness that a non-Christian experiences, it is unfortunately limited in quality and it's only temporary. The facts are anyone without the saving grace of Jesus, is spiritually dead. A person cannot live the "full life" if they are spiritually dead. The Bible says, Ephesians 2:4 *"God, who is rich in mercy, made us alive with Christ (even when we were dead)."* If you are in Christ, the abundant life is waiting for you! There is the answer. It's waiting, like a Christmas present under the tree with YOUR name written on the gift tag! Just for you.

4. God is inviting you to experience an 'Abundant Life'.

1 Timothy 6:17 says *"...God richly provides us with everything for our enjoyment."* Read that again. That means that it is God's desire that all His children discover happiness and satisfaction in this life. Unfortunately, many Christians are still missing out on the fullness of life. Perhaps, they do not believe that such a life is truly available to them.

Notice in John 10:10 that Jesus didn't say, *"I come that SOME may have life to the full".* Nope. It says that "you" may have life to the fullest.

You. Write your name in there above that verse. You. All believers are invited to discover abundant living. It is available to all God's children, no matter what their circumstances are in life. This is a hard concept for many Christians to accept.

Many assume the abundant life depends on circumstances, or fate or luck, or their bank account, or their status in life, or their health. No doubt, these things are highly valued in our lives, but Jesus said in Luke 16:14, *"What is highly valued among men is detestable in God's sight."* Wealth, power, status, and worldly pleasure have nothing to do with living the full life. What does that mean to us? It means that life should be full of excitement, vibrant, passion and enjoyment. We have a Savior! We should be the most positive people on the face of the earth. But unfortunately, we lose that taste for life quickly and become, once again, dead.

How do we keep from becoming "dead" again? In Romans 12:11-13 it says, *"Never be lacking in zeal, but keep your spiritual fervor, serving the Lord. Be joyful in hope, patient in affliction, faithful in prayer. Share with God's people who are in need. Practice hospitality."*

I have to confess that I'm not the brightest crayon in the box or the sharpest knife in the drawer, BUT this isn't rocket science here. These are a few wonderful ways to bring life back into your lifeless world. Let's look at several of these practical keys found in the above scripture over the next few days.

When you start to experience apathy or boredom in your life, what do you do? Look at verse 11. *"Never be lacking in zeal"*. What is zeal? Eagerness. Excitement. Enthusiasm. The word enthusiasm comes from two words, "en-theos." "Theos" means God. The more in God you are, the more enthusiastic you will be. Christ must have had that kind of excitement in His life and work. He always was positive and eager to do the next thing. He would have never accepted "we don't have time" or "we've never done it that way before" Christian mentality.

Although we are going to dive into Colossians a little later in the book, let me give you a short preview of what Colossians 3:23 says, *"Whatever you do, work at it with all your heart, as working for the Lord and not for men."*

So when boredom, complacency, apathy....death, starts to sneak in to our lives, what do we need to do? The above verses tell us to fight off signs of death with enthusiasm. Excitement. Zeal. I think the Lord scoots to the edge of his throne when we looks down and sees one of His children getting excited. When is the last time you have got excited for the Lord? When is the last time you have been filled with enthusiasm for living for the Lord?

Not just enthusiasm, but spiritual excitement. Break out of the death. Break out of the grave! Break out! Today is the beginning of your spiritual resurrection. Remember the words of one of my favorite hymns by Alfred H. Ackley, "I serve a risen Savior, He's in the world today. I know that He is living whatever men may say. I see His hand of mercy, I hear His voice of cheer. Just the time I need Him, He's always near. He Lives!"

Don't you think it's time that you should start to live, too?

WRITTEN IN STONE

THE COWBOY'S PRAYER

Oh Lord, I reckon I'm not much just by myself.
I fail to do a lot of things I ought to do.
But Lord, when trails are steep and passes high,
Help me to ride it straight the whole way through.
And when in the falling dusk I get the final call,
I do not care how many flowers they send--
Above all else the happiest trail would be
For You to say to me, "Let's ride, My friend."
Amen

Roy Rogers
located in Sunset Hills Memorial
Park, Apple Valley, California

FINAL WORDS

A dying man can do nothing easy.
--Benjamin Franklin, statesman, died April 17, 1790

CHAPTER 3
Faces of Death

"The opposite of love is not hate, it's indifference.
The opposite of art is not ugliness, it's indifference.
The opposite of faith is not heresy, it's indifference.
The opposite of life is not death, it's indifference."

-Elie Wiesel

Look around. How many people do you experience throughout the day that are just enduring life? Faces of death everywhere you look. Everywhere you go. At work, at the post office, at our favorite diner... death. Faces of death. Now with that thought in mind, put down the book and go look at yourself in the mirror. What do you see?

Wait. Don't leave so soon. Keep looking. Go ahead and go back to the mirror and don't just glance. Look. Look into your own eyes. This is the time not to point the finger at everybody else and the way they live or should I say, "don't live". This is a serious time of reflection. Does your face resemble death or does it reflect the love of Christ through it with excitement and fire?

I have found over the years that it becomes so easy to mask over what we really are and try to put on a face that we think others want to see. But it's not real. It's fake. It's lifeless. Faces of death.

How much of the presence of God is being allowed to flow through your life? What do other people see in you? Christ? Death? Apathy?

As we continue to look at Romans 12:11-13, look at the last part of verse 11, *"but keep your spiritual fervor."* This literally means that we should have a fire for Jesus. That we should be so fired up for the Lord that everyone around us can see you glowing for Jesus. What is this fire for the Lord? Well, let hear what Jesus says about it in Luke 12:49, *"I have come to bring fire on the earth, and how I wish it were already kindled."* What the Lord is simply saying is that "I want you to be so excited and fired up with the glory and presence of God that when people look at you, they will see you glowing." Is that what they see? Is that what you see?

The problem with the fire for the Lord is that there are so many "cold water committees" and people that feel they have been selected by God to "correct" those on-fire Christians. Our society has become a society that downplays excitement for the Lord. Even fellow believers will use everything in their power to keep the excited and enthusiastic in their proper places. Why? Because it threatens their comfort zone. If you'll just be boring and dead along with them, they will feel so much better. Don't fall for this trick used by Satan anymore.

Breakout! Get fired up! Charles Spurgeon was one of the greatest preachers in England. A young preacher came to Spurgeon and asked him, "How can I have the same impact that you're having?" Charles Spurgeon said, "Simple. Pour gasoline over your body, light a match, and people will come and watch you burn for Jesus."

Burn for Jesus. What a wonderful thought.

The words found in the Luke 12:49 passage "bring fire" is a phrase that means to "cast fire" or to "throw fire." Jesus came to be a holy flamethrower! The fire He is speaking of is not literal fire but a spiritual fire. He is speaking of the burning, exciting, dynamic presence of God in the lives of people. I want to show you from scripture what this fire is and what it can do in your life.

1. The Fire Symbolizes God's Awesome Presence.

When God appeared to Moses He spoke out of the flame of a burning bush. Later, on Mt. Sinai, God appeared to all the Israelites as a fire on the mountain. Exodus 24:17 says, *"To the Israelites, the glory of the Lord looked like a consuming fire."* What a sight that must have been! Later, when Moses built the Tabernacle, they made the first sacrifice in the Holy of Holies. God again revealed Himself by fire. Leviticus 9:24 says, *"Fire came out from the presence of the Lord and consumed the burnt offering ... And when all the people saw it, they shouted for joy and fell face-down."*

Remember the movie when Moses (aka Charlton Heston) was descending from the mountain after spending some intimate time with the Master? What did the people see in Moses? A glow. A fire. A radiant light beaming from within coming out through his eyes and face.

Probably one of the best explanations of what Jesus is talking about is found in the New Testament when John the Baptist was asked if he was the Messiah he replied, *"I baptize you with water. But one more powerful than I will come, the thongs of whose sandals I am not worthy to untie. He will baptize you with the Holy Spirit and with fire."* (Luke 3:16) Jesus came to totally immerse people in the burning, purifying, awesome presence of God. That's why He came to bring fire on the earth. When you have a personal encounter with the God of the Universe, it's like an experience with Holy Fire. On the first Easter, those two disciples walked with the resurrection Jesus on the road to Emmaus. They didn't recognize that it was Jesus because they were certain He was dead and buried. After Jesus revealed Himself and disappeared they said, *"Were not our hearts burning within us while He talked with us?"* (Luke 24:32)

When your heart is on fire for someone; that means you are passionate about that person. Jesus came to give us that kind of burning, passionate, love relationship with the God of the Universe.

2. The Fire Symbolizes God's Unlimited Power.

Do you know why so many people are walking around your community with depressed, lifeless, faces of death? It's because they aren't allowing the unlimited power of the Master of the Universe burning throughout their hearts and lives.

Jesus mentioned in Acts 1:8 *"You will receive power after the Holy Spirit has come upon you."* The Holy Spirit living in you is like the fire of God that generates the power you need to live the Christian life. He gives you power to share your faith or to forgive people who have hurt you, or to love unlovely people. In your own strength you can't live the Christian life. Jesus said, in John 5:5 *"Without Me you can do nothing."* But the fire of God in your heart will be like a spark that generates the energy you need to live the Christian life.

Fire will only keep burning as long as it has fuel and oxygen, but when it runs out of either, it will go out. Now, God is eternal, but the power He provides us is not something we can just take for granted as always being there. We must tend the fire in order to keep it burning.

If you don't tend a fire, it will simply burn itself out. The sad thing is, this can also happen spiritually. The sad reality of many Christians is that we have replaced the fiery, dynamic Christian life for some kind of dispassionate, mediocre substitute.

The Apostle Paul wrote in I Thessalonians 5:19. *"Don't put out the Spirit's fire."* Have you allowed that to be done in your life? Spiritual fervor and fire can be extinguished by simple apathy. If you neglect prayer, Bible Study, your quiet time, or regular fellowship with other Christians, the fire will go out. You don't lose your salvation; you lose the joy of your salvation. You lose your zeal, your edge and your fervor.

Has your fire gone out? This is why fellowship with other believers is so vitally important. Read the following e-mail I just received from one the deacons from my church, Hugh Lehnen, this evening. It goes like this:

A certain church member, who had previously been attending church regularly, stopped going. After a few weeks, the pastor decided to visit him.

It was a chilly evening. The pastor found the man at home alone, sitting before a blazing fire. Guessing the reason for his pastor's visit, the man welcomed him, led him to a comfortable chair near the fireplace and waited.

The pastor made himself at home but said nothing. In the silence, he contemplated the dance of the flames around the burning logs.

After some minutes, the pastor took the fire tongs, carefully picked up a brightly burning ember and placed it to one side of the hearth all alone, then sat back in his chair, still silent.

The host watched all this in quiet contemplation. As the one lone ember's flame flickered and diminished, there was a momentary glow and then its fire was no more. Soon it was cold and dead.

Not a word had been spoken since the initial greeting. The pastor glanced at his watch and realized it was time to leave.

He slowly stood up, picked up the cold, dead ember and placed it back in the middle of the fire. Immediately it began to glow once more with the light and warmth of the burning coals around it.

As the pastor reached the door to leave, his host said with a tear running down his cheek, "Thank you so much for your visit, and especially for the fiery sermon. I shall be back in church next Sunday."

Has the fire gone out? If it has, this is God's way of telling you it is time to re-ignite your zeal and fervor for Him. Surround yourself with the people that help "fan the flames." Stay away from the crowds that are carrying the buckets of cold water.

3. The Fire Will Capture the Attention of People.

Fire has an amazing quality. People will drive from miles around to watch something burn. It captures the attention of people and they are fascinated by the power and intensity of the flames. Hummmmm. Could there be a spiritual parallel here? Don't miss it! People will be drawn to you and the church if there is FIRE BURNING FROM WITHIN. This world is craving that fire.

Watch this. That's exactly what happened on the Day of Pentecost. A group of Christians got on fire for Jesus and the crowds came to check it out. Acts 2:3, 6, 12 says: *"When the day of Pentecost came ... they saw what seemed to be tongues of fire that separated and came to rest on each of them. All of them were filled with the Holy Spirit and began to speak in other tongues ... when they heard this sound, a crowd came together in bewilderment ... amazed and perplexed, they asked one another, "What does this mean?"*

God gave each believer a little flame–and when the folks in Jerusalem heard what was happening, they came to check out the fire. 3,000 of them were saved and baptized that very day. 5.000 others were saved a few days later. A good fire attracts a crowd.

Remember this little nugget of truth. God doesn't set churches on fire. He ignites individuals. At Pentecost, each believer had his own little fire, and when they put them together they had a church on fire.

When you've got this fire, you can't keep it inside! Jeremiah wrote in Jeremiah 20:9 *"His word is in my heart like a fire, a fire shut up in my bones. I am weary of holding it in; indeed I cannot."* He just had to allow the Holy Spirit Flamethrower to shoot this fire onto others.

The New Testament tells us our bodies are the temples of the Holy Spirit. Wouldn't you love to have the fire of God fall in your heart and for His glory to fill this temple? Sure you would! Trade in your face of death for an illuminated and glowing face that reflects the power and presence of a vibrant and living Lord.

You may be asking, "How can I do that?" First, admit the fire is gone out. Next, refuse to be a cool, apathetic believer. Finally, simply ask God to relight your fire.

WRITTEN IN STONE

A master of comedy
His genius in the art of humor
Brought gladness
To the world he loved.

Stan Laurel
located in Forest Lawn; Hollywood
Hills, Los Angeles, California

FINAL WORDS

Turn up the lights, I don't want to go home in the dark.

-- O. Henry (William Sidney Porter),
writer, died June 4, 1910

CHAPTER 4
DOA

*"There are worse things in life than death.
Have you ever spent an evening with an insurance salesman?"*
-Woody Allen

DOA. Dead on arrival. That means before they got to their desire location, death set in. Now in a believer's life several things can cause the death process to begin. Many things, like heartbreak, sickness, divorce, loss of a job, and the list goes on and on that causes our life to ebb away. How do we handle this brokenness?

The answer will be revealed as we continue looking in our verses in Romans 12:11-13 and focus on verse 12: *"Be joyful in hope, patient in affliction, faithful in prayer."* The Bible tells us here that affliction will come. Count on it. I guarantee it.

You have no control over when, where and what kind troubles hit you. The one thing that you can control is how you are going to react to the problems. This verse says several things that you should do when you're facing a major problem in your life.

First thing, <u>look beyond the problem and rejoice in the Lord</u>. That is exactly what verse 12 is telling us when it says, "be joyful in hope." Rejoice in the Lord. No matter the circumstances, rejoice. How in the world do you rejoice when your world is caving in all around you? The key to this verse is found in the word "hope." Hope is the very item that will allow you to get out of bed in the morning. There is hope. This is the only way that rejoicing will ever be present during your trials. Hope.

No matter what your circumstance, no matter what your trial or tribulation that you are going through right now, rejoice! So reach down deep inside of yourself, grab yourself by your ol' bootstraps and rejoice.

The second thing that this verse tells us is that throughout the affliction or trial, <u>you must have patience</u>. Patience is a virtue that doesn't mean that you should just sit and wait. The patience that is spoken of here is an active belief that the Lord will work all things out for His glory. Patience produces character. Patience produces a dependence on the Lord. A dependence that only He can fulfill. I can't even program my DVD recorder on my television set. How can I tell the Creator of the Universe how or when to handle my problems? I need to depend completely on His knowledge and wisdom. Listen to James 1:2-3, *"Consider it joy whenever you face trials of many kinds, because you know that the testing of your faith develops perseverance."* Patience.

There is an awesome poem from an unknown author that speaks of patience and the little things that irritate us in this world. It goes like this:

THE OYSTER

There once was an oyster whose story I tell,
Who found that sand had got under his shell,
Just one little grain, but it gave him much pain,
For oysters have feelings, although they're so plain.
Now, did he berate the working of fate,
Which led him to such a deplorable state?
Did he curse out the government
Or call for election? No.
As he lay on the shelf,
He said to himself,
If I cannot remove it,
I'll try to improve it.

So the years rolled by,
As the years always do,
And he came to his ultimate destiny-oyster stew.
And this small grain of sand
Which had bothered him so,
Was a beautiful pearl,
All richly aglow.

Now, this tale has a moral,
For isn't it grand,
What an oyster can do.
With a morsel of sand?
What couldn't we do
If we'd only begin
With all of the things
That get under our skin.

So just when you are ready to throw in the towel and throw your hands up and say "I'm done", remember to Rejoice in the hope of the Lord and hang onto your patience. That irritant will be a pearl someday.

The final thing that is mentioned is to be <u>"faithful in prayer"</u>. Never, ever stop praying. Prayer is our lifeline of spiritual oxygen that allows us to live even when death surrounds us. Pray for the power to rejoice in trials, patience in tribulation and a passionate prayer life to continue to keep your heart from becoming dead.

Everything in our society today fights against prayer. Our busy lives interfere with times of prayer. Between cell phones, blackberries, internet, and television, we are constantly being bombarded with stuff that really doesn't amount to a hill of beans. What this "stuff" does accomplish is that it keeps us from time alone with God. It keeps us busy. But Society tells us that if we aren't always on the go that we aren't successful.

Now there is no specific formula for how we should pray. One of the things that make prayer so great is that there is no right or wrong way to pray. However in order for us not to become stagnant in our prayer life and in order for us to be as spiritually nourished as possible, there are some guidelines I'd like to share with you about how to pray. Some of you have probably heard of different prayer plans to follow, but I find this one to be the most well rounded. This plan utilizes five words to guide your prayer life.

The first is CONFESSION. 1 John 1:9, *"If we confess our sins, he is faithful and just and will forgive us our sins and purify us from all unrighteousness."* You should confess all known sin in your life when you start in prayer so that you can open the channel of communication with you and God. If you try to hide your sin from God or simply ignore it, you put up a roadblock in your communication with God.

As you confess your sins to God, ask God to look into your heart and reveal sins to you that you may not be aware of.

After confession comes PRAISE. 1 Chronicles 29:10-13, *"David praised the Lord in the presence of the whole assembly, saying, 'Praise be to you, O Lord, God of our father Israel, from everlasting to everlasting. Yours, O Lord, is the greatness and the power and the glory and the majesty and the splendor, for everything in heaven and earth is yours. Yours, O Lord, is the kingdom; you are exalted as head over all. Wealth and honor come from you; you are the ruler of all things. In your hands are strength and power to exalt and give strength to all. Now, our God, we give you thanks, and praise your glorious name."*

After you have been cleansed of your sin, it is a good time to give praise to God. Praise expresses our love and adoration for our heavenly father. As you praise God, focus your thoughts on his greatness, power, majesty, grace, mercy, and unending love for you. Use a scripture such as the one above to focus your praise on God.

After praise comes THANKSGIVING. It says in 1 Thessalonians 5:18, *"Give thanks in all circumstances, for this is God's will for you in Christ Jesus."* Every day of our life we have something for which we can be thankful for. We can thank God for our health, our safety, our friends, family, church, joyful times in our life, and of course for our salvation.

After thanksgiving comes INTERCESSION. 1 Timothy 2:1-4, *"I urge, then, first of all, that requests, prayers, intercession and thanksgiving be made for everyone, for kings and all those in authority, that we may live peaceful and quiet lives in all godliness and holiness. This is good, and pleases God our Savior, who wants all men to be saved and to come to a knowledge of the truth."* This means that we are responsible to pray for others. How many of you have enthusiastically promised to pray for someone and then forgotten to do so? We should pray regularly for our pastors, our government leaders, our missionaries, our friends, and our family. We should especially pray for those who are in need with physical or emotional problems. We should pray for others in the same way that we pray for ourselves. God will meet the needs of others if we pray for them, just as he meets our own needs.

The final point to our plan of prayer is PETITION. Mark 11:24, *"Therefore I tell you, whatever you ask for in prayer, believe that you have received it, and it will be yours."* We need to pray for ourselves and our personal needs. Whatever these may be, we can bring them to God and expect him to answer. We should pray for specific things for which we can expect specific answers. A faithful prayer is one you expect God to hear and to answer, it is also a prayer that is unselfish and seeking God's will and not your own. A prayer of petition is not meant for our own selfish needs, but to help us meet the needs that God desires and to do his will.

Through all of these things reveal to God your requests and let them be made known to Him, but do so with a humble heart truly seeking His will. In all things pray without ceasing.

We all have problems, issues, stress and tragedies that we need to deal with. How are you coping? How are you dealing with the stress? Don't allow it to "snuff" out your light and life.

The only time that you're going to get rid of all the problems in your life is when you're in a coffin buried in a cemetery. In life trouble is guaranteed, but misery is optional. The choice is yours and the way you approach the problems in your life will determine whether you are miserable or not. Don't arrive DOA years before you give up your last breath. Think about it.

WRITTEN IN STONE

My Jesus Mercy
Alphonse Capone
located in Mt. Carmel Cemetery; Chicago, Illinois

FINALS WORDS

It is very beautiful over there.
--Thomas Alva Edison, inventor, died October 18, 1931

CHAPTER 5
Rigor Mortis

"If you spend all your time worrying about death,
Living isn't going to be much fun."
-From the TV show "Rosanne"

Rigor mortis: a temporary stiffening of muscles occurring after death. Hummmm, a temporary stiffening after death. What causes this stiffening? Death. The lack of living blood flowing through your body keeping it alive.

In the physical body what causes the blood to stop flowing to certain areas? It could be a blockage, high cholesterol, hardening of the arteries or many other problems. The spiritual heart can be affected in the same manner forcing certain parts of our body to stiffen or harden. I call it spiritual cholesterol.

God's Word expresses this spiritual cholesterol problem in Matthew 13:15, *"For this people's heart has become calloused; their ears are hard of hearing, and they have closed their eyes. Otherwise they might see with their eyes, hear with their ears, understand with their hearts and turn, and I would heal them."*

The wonderful book of Proverbs 28:14 puts it this way, *"Blessed is the man who always fears the Lord, but he who hardens his heart falls into trouble."*

Here's what the gospel of Mark says in chapter 16, verse 14, *"Later He appeared to the eleven as they sat at the table; and He rebuked their unbelief and hardness of the heart."* Ouch! The risen Lord is talking to his "faithful" disciples and land blasting them for their lack of faith and hardening of their hearts. The very disciples that walked with Him every day for the three years of Jesus' ministry on this earth even had trouble with their spiritual cholesterol.

What caused this spiritual cholesterol to build up so fast in the disciples? Too many fish dinners cooked in high cholesterol oil of Jerusalem? No. Too much manna dipped in honey sauce from Galilee? Nope. How about brokenness? They had their hearts broken. Their entire world had just recently been turned upside down and they didn't know how to react to it.

Sound familiar? Just when everything is comfortable and all the bills are paid, something happens and your world starts to shake. Just when you think the family if finally doing fine and dandy, the phone rings and it's the local police station wanting to discuss your son's behavior over the weekend. Just when your marriage couldn't be more secure, papers arrive in the mail to your office from your wife announcing the promise of a divorce. Or could it be that the one person in this world that you should be able to trust, your father, has spent the last several years abusing you in a way that could never be described.

That's when the spiritual cholesterol starts to clog every artery in your brain and heart causing a stiffness and hardness that you have never experienced before. Your reaction to the condition of your spiritual heart problems can bring you out of death or quickly shut the coffin lid on your hopes and dreams of ever experiencing life again.

I want to express to you today that spiritual cholesterol can happen to the very best of us. But this heart problem is one of the most serious and dangerous condition of them all. In the physical realm it is a number one priority with some folks to make sure they eat the right foods and keep their cholesterol under control. Then in the same breath make no indication or care that their spiritual cholesterol is soaring by the day and heading for a heart attack of major consequences. We need to be even more concerned about our spiritual hearts and its condition.

Let me try to explain this spiritual hardening of the heart. It doesn't happen in an instant. Hardening of the spiritual heart is a gradual process that can take months or even years to happen. But once it does occur, beware. It can be deadly.

How do we avoid such a condition? Look at Psalm 95:1-7, *"Come, let us sing for joy to the Lord; let us shout aloud to the Rock of our salvation. Let us come before him with thanksgiving and extol him with music and song. For the Lord is the great God, the great King above all gods. In his hand are the depths of the earth, and the mountain peaks belong to him. The sea is his, for he made it, and his hands formed the dry land. Come, let us bow down in worship, let us kneel before the Lord our Maker, for he is our God and we are the people of his pasture, the flock under his care."*

So far so good. This is a sweet piece of scripture and the priests were calling everyone and inviting them to worship God, but in the back of the congregation maybe one of the priests saw that grumpy, grouchy, old prune with that look on his face that said, "Do we have to? Surely we're not going to sing those same old songs again are we? When is this church service going to be over? Hurry up so I can go get something to eat."

Does this attitude ever creep into your mentality at church or during your quiet time with the Lord? For some, it has been that same attitude for years that has caused the heart problem. That's could be the very reason that the Psalm continues with verse 8, *"Today, if you hear his voice, do not harden your hearts as you did at Meribah, as you did that day at Massah in the desert, where your fathers tested and tried me, though they had seen what I did. For forty years I was angry with that generation; I said, "They are a people whose hearts go astray, and they have not known my ways." So I declared on oath in my anger, They shall never enter my rest."*

The psalmist is making reference to what their forefathers did in Exodus 17. You remember the story (or at least saw the movie) about how the Israelites were freed from Egypt, crossed through the Red Sea on dry ground and then God supplies them with box lunches each day of manna and quail to eat. But then, watch this, all of a sudden they get bored and thirsty.

Exodus 17:1-7, *"The whole Israelite community set out from the Desert of Sin, traveling from place to place as the Lord commanded. They camped at Rephidim, but there was no water for the people to drink. So they quarreled with Moses and said, "Give us water to drink." Moses replied, "Why do you quarrel with me? Why do you put the Lord to the test?" But the people were thirsty for water there, and they grumbled against Moses. They said, "Why did you bring us up out of Egypt to make us and our children and livestock die of thirst?" Then Moses cried out to the Lord, "What am I to do with these people? They are almost ready to stone me." The Lord answered Moses, "Walk on ahead of the people. Take with you some of the elders of Israel and take in your hand the staff with which you struck the Nile, and go. I will stand there before you by the rock at Horeb. Strike the rock, and water will come out of it for the people to drink." So Moses did this in the sight of the elders of Israel. And he called the place Massah and Meribah because the Israelites quarreled and because they tested the Lord saying, "Is the Lord among us or not?"*

I can find in the above verses several warning signs of spiritual cholesterol.

1) Excessive Griping.

Phillippians 2:14, *"Do all things without complaining and arguing."* Does this describe you? Phillippians says, "do all things" without griping. All things. All. Need I say more? There are many people in this world that feel that have been hand selected by the Lord to be His critical mouthpiece regarding everything in life, work and church. The Israelites only needed to look down at the wrist and ankles and realize that the chains were gone. They were free and no longer slaves to Egypt, but they couldn't see past their daily wants and desires.

They weren't only complaining about Moses but in reality they were complaining about the Lord. They were saying, "God, is this the best you can do?"

2) Excessive Doubting.

James 1:6, *"But let him ask in faith without any doubting, because he who doubts is like a wave of the sea, blown and tossed by the wind."* The entire point of this story lets us in to why God was so upset with them. They doubted God. God wanted them to have the faith that He would provide like He had done so many times before and even over and above their wildest imaginations.

The hardening of the spiritual heart is a disease that can result in the death of your faith. Because slowly but surely, you just don't trust God anymore. There are Christians that have hardened their hearts and decided to walk away from God or to at least doubt God's ability to help them.

Is that you? How long has it been since you've had a spiritual cholesterol check? Don't fear, the next chapter will give you a few cures for the spiritual hardening of the heart so that the rigor mortis don't start setting in on your heart and prevent it from beating for the Lord.

WRITTEN IN STONE

Truth and History.
21 Men.
The Boy Bandit King --
He Died As He Lived.

William H. Bonney "Billy the Kid"
located in Fort Sumner Cemetery;
Fort Sumner New Mexico

FINAL WORDS

I am ready.
--Woodrow Wilson, US President, died 1924

CHAPTER 6
A Matter of Life or Death

"Let us endeavor to live that when we come to die
Even the undertake will be sorry."
-Mark Twain

After reading the previous chapter about spiritual cholesterol, you maybe be realizing that some death has entered into your heart and life and you would like to take a few moments to clean it out.

Good news. There is a cure for the hardening of the heart. Bad news. It's not found in a bottle of spiritual "Draino" that with just one swig and all of your crud will be flushed down the pipes. The cure for the disease and potential death is the same cure as if you were seeing a medical doctor about your physical cholesterol.

The doc would probably ask you a few questions about your behavior, habits and lifestyle. Do you smoke? What about the foods you eat? Are you involved in an exercise program? (Oh by the way, just sitting and watching the "Biggest Loser" on TV doesn't qualify as a medically endorsed physical regiment.)

The same with the spiritual and you won't even have to take off your clothes and put on a hospital gown. Let's look first at your diet.

What are you eating? What kind of spiritual diet do we need to have? What are some things we need to be careful to put into our bodies that may cause spiritual cholesterol?

Make sure that you are getting a healthy diet of spiritual food that will build the muscles of faith and relationship with the Lord. Not just a weekly meal at church, but a daily dose of rich and calcium-filled Word of the Lord. There aren't any pills or potions that can substitute the Word of God in your life. Jesus called it the "bread of life" for a reason…it will sustain life within you and your family.

But is reading the Word enough? The Pharisees read the Word and even had the words memorized in their heads, but became arrogant and flashy with their knowledge and didn't let the message affect them on the inside. 1 Corinthians 10:12 warns us, *"Therefore let him who thinks he stand take heed lest he falls."*

We must keep an eye on what we are eating and what we are filling our spiritual bellies full of. It was said, "We are what we eat." There is a lot of truth in that statement in the physical and spiritual realm.

The next cure for spiritual cholesterol is in our exercise. It's easy to understand how we can let our physical bodies start to deteriorate over the years and our bellies start rolling over our belts. Every time you step onto your talking bathroom scales it says, "One at a time, please." The condition of our spiritual body is even more important.

1 Timothy 4:6-8 says, *"If you point these things out to the brothers, you will be a good minister of Christ Jesus, brought up in the truths of the faith and of the good teaching that you have followed. Have nothing to do with godless myths and old wives' tales; rather,* ***train yourself to be godly****. For physical training is of some value, but godliness has value for all things, holding promise for both the present life and the life to come."*

The main nugget of truth in the above scripture is the command to *"train yourself to be godly."* I love a couple of the other scripture translations on this section of God's Word. The Living Bible puts it this way: *"spend your time and energy in the exercise of becoming spiritually fit."* But the most AWESOME version of this is found in The Message, it says, *"Exercise daily in God-no spiritual flabbiness, please!"* Yes! Perfect! I understand that kind of talking.

Famous NFL Football Coach, Mike Ditka had a famous quote that goes like this: "I don't believe that anything is unrealistic if you believe you can do it. I think if you are determined enough and willing to pay the price you can get it done." This success just doesn't happen overnight.

Just like a diet….it takes time, endurance and determination. Go ahead, "train yourself to be godly". Engage in the regular exercise of the soul and spirit that brings a condition and a healthier inner person.

The one thing that will give you an edge and keep you "full of life" is a daily input and exercising of the Word of God in your life. We spend so much time filling our lives, minds and spirits with non-Christian nonsense. We jump on the latest version of a self-success plan called "The Secret" like it is the way out of our daily grind of being lifeless. Here is another nugget of truth: "The Secret" is no secret. It can be found in the very Word of God. Turn off the television, mute Oprah, and focus on the almighty God. Now, THAT'S the secret!!!!

It seems to me that there has been a general "dumbing down" in our society to what the Word of God teaches us. George Barna made a shocking statement in one of his latest books, "One half of Americans are functionally illiterate; unable to read the scripture with understanding and unable to comprehend the sermons that we are preaching."

Are we somehow less capable than our grandparents or have we simply allowed our brains to become "flabby" because we fail to practice the disciple of studying God's Word? This is a matter of life or death. No doubt.

Jesus Christ said in John 8:31-32, *"If you hold to My teaching, you are really my disciples. Then you will know the truth, and the truth will set you free."*

You want life? You want to experience freedom? God's Word makes it clear throughout scripture that we must work out with our faith and have the endurance of a marathon runner just to make it through this world victorious. The neat thing about this type of exercise is that we can jump right into it right now. We don't have to wait until the next New Year celebration to make a resolution to start exercising for the Lord. The spiritual exercising can begin today.

Is your heart starting to slow down because of the lack of blood flowing through it? The blood that is flowing through your spiritual body contains the very elements that keep us alive. Start eating the right things, exercising your faith, prayers and beliefs right now.

It is a matter of the heart. It is a matter of life and death.

WRITTEN IN STONE

The Body of
B. Franklin, Printer
Like the Cover of an old Book
Its Contents turn out
And Stript of its Lettering & Guilding
Lies here. Food for Worms
For, it will as he believed
appear once more
In a new and more elegant Edition
corrected and improved
By the Author
Benjamin Franklin
located at Christ Church Burial Grounds;
Philadelphia, Pennsylvania

FINAL WORDS

Don't let it end like this. Tell them I said something.
--Pancho Villa, Mexican revolutionary, died 1923

CHAPTER 7
Dead Calm

"The idea is to die young as late as possible."
-Ashley Montagu

REFLECTION AND REVIEW DAY.

God Himself laid down a foundation of taking a day off per week to recharge, reflect and review the week. The idea of this is carried on throughout this book. Take some extra time today to sit and think about the following questions and thoughts and how they impact you and your life.

Chapter 1: "A Trip to the Morgue"

*Describe your experience in your place of worship.

____

____

____

____

*What are the characteristics that reflect life in your worship service?

____

____

____

____

*What are the characteristics that more resemble death in your church?

____

____

____

____

Chapter 2: I See Dead People"

*Read John 10:10 again and indicate what life you are experiencing.

____

____

____

____

*What areas of your walk with the Lord indicate that you are experiencing His fullness for you?

____

____

____

____

*What areas did you need to work on to receive the fullness of the Lord?

____

____

____

____

Chapter 3: "Faces of Death"

*What did you see in the mirror?

*List the things that more resemble death than life in your relationship with the Jesus.

Chapter 4: DOA"

*What is your first reaction when a problem occurs in your life?

*Is it difficult for you to rejoice in the time of troubles?

*What area of your life does patience seem to be lacking?

Chapter 5: 'Rigor Mortis'

*What part of your heart (life) has experienced hardening?

____

____

____

____

*What situation has life handed you that caused you to experience brokenness?

____

____

____

____

*Think about your areas of "griping" and "doubting".

____

____

____

Chapter 6: "A Matter of Life or Death"

*What does your spiritual diet consist of?

*How about your spiritual exercise activity that you are giving God? Journal your thoughts and your feelings about the first week of readings:

WRITTEN IN STONE

...that nothing's so sacred as honor and nothing's so loyal as love
Wyatt Earp
located in Hills of Eternity; Colma, California

FINAL WORDS

Is it the Fourth?
-- Thomas Jefferson, US President, d. July 4, 1826

CHAPTER 8
1st Community Church of the Comatose

"It is foolish and wrong to mourn the men who died. Rather we should thank God that such men lived."
-George S. Patton, Jr.

In the world today over 56,500,000 people die each year. Which figures to about 155,000 people a day, 6,458 an hour, and 108 people per minute. Which means every second 2 people die. For every breath you take approximately seven people have died. Death is everywhere, and it happens to everyone.

Did you hear about the church that was so dead that when a church member actually died in a service that the paramedics carried out 5 people before they got the right one?

Experts in the paramedic field every day in the United States arrive on the scene of accidents where the victim has crossed over the barrier between life and death. There is no heartbeat. The respiratory system's breathing has stopped. All the vital signs of life are gone. But the paramedics do not accept this death as final. They immediately begin CPR, perhaps inject a special drug designed to stimulate the heart. For a few frantic moments, nothing happens. Then, out of nowhere, the victim begins to cough, taking a few shallow breaths, and then the heart begins to beat, pulsing life through the body. So instead of sending the corpse to the morgue, the ambulance takes the patient to the hospital. Here's the $64,000 question: Was the victim dead?

Without getting too theological or technical, we would have to answer, yes. If not for the expert knowledge and care of the experienced paramedics, the accident would have been followed by a funeral. But we have all heard stories that in many instances, this kind of death doesn't have to be final. With the proper stimulus, the person can be revived. Once flat lined....now a vibrant and active heart!

The problem today is that churches all over the United States are in major need of Spiritual CPR. The vital signs are slowing to almost a complete standstill. The heartbeat of the church has been slowly declining each and every year in hundreds of thousand sanctuaries across this land. We have come upon the self-made accident and desperately need a skilled team of paramedics to perform their work on the body.

One of the biggest obstacles that the church must face is that the local spiritual body of the church doesn't always necessarily look dead. They are sitting in dead churches, worshipping with dead-so-called Christians, listening to dead sermons week after week from a dead-head preacher. No salvations. No miracles. No answered prayers. No life.

The scary thing is that appearances can be so deceiving. From the outside the buildings look so nice. Fancy stained glass windows. A beautiful steeple. On the inside the fanciest carpets and padded pews are installed. Each member has the newest edition of the New King James Version of the Bible that has special recipes to be used for special fellowships between each book. All church members are required to have their hair done on Saturday morning so they will look their best on Sunday morning.

You know the church that I'm talking about. When you walk in the door everyone turns and stares at you and evaluates your "Sunday best" on a scale of 1 to 10 and votes on the special ballots that have been inserted in the bulletin. The church, that when a baby cries or a child ruffles papers, everyone glares at them hoping the parents will get the "hint" to remove the disturbance from amongst the saints.

Let's not leave out the pastor. When he enters from the side door of the platform, his long and elaborate robe flows in the breeze but not too strong so his hair won't be blown out of place. When he opens his mouth, he uses language that includes "thee," "thine," and "thou." Majority of the congregation couldn't tell you what the sermon was about for a free lunch every Sunday for a year at the local buffet. He pronounces Christ's name with an extra syllable, "Lord-da" and concludes his infinitely long prayer with a resounding "Amen-ah". You know the type of church I'm talking about.

I'm so afraid that we make our Lord and Savior sick to His precious stomach each Sunday when we "play the game." I don't feel that this was what Christ had in mind when He spoke of His Bride. I wonder what He is thinking when He looks down on us each Sunday at 10:30 am. Would it bring a smile to His face or a tear to His eyes?

How about the offering? This is the type of church that collects all they can, cans all they collect, and then sit on the can. They seek to gather all the money that is available without letting any of it back into the community to help a family that can't afford to eat a decent meal that lives across the street from the church. The church that is more interested in their investments at the local bank instead of their investments in the needy children of the community and world.

This is what I call Body Bag Religion. Dead and they just don't know it.

Before I go any further and deeper, take a break right now. Set this book down and dwell on the reality of what your individual church truly is. Take an inventory of the good, the bad and the ugly. Be realistic and cut through all the make-up and get down to the real heart of the Body. In your mind scroll down the list of programs and activities that are conducted each and every week at your church. Decide if they are designed and have the heart to point people to Christ.

Take a real and close examination of the Body at the scene of the accident. Do you feel a pulse? Is the heart beating or fading into a near comatose state? Does the Body need CPR now before it's too late?

WRITTEN IN STONE

"The Entertainer"
He did it all
Sammy Davis, Jr.
located in Forest Lawn; Glendale, California

FINAL WORDS

A King should die standing.
--Louis XVIII, King of France, died 1824

CHAPTER 9
House of 1,000 Corpses

"I have offended God and mankind because my work didn't reach the quality it should have."
-Last words of Leonardo da Vinci

Church growth professionals have researched the lives of thousands of churches all over the world and have concluded that most churches go through four stages of life. They can be classified in the following groups:

1) Movement Stage. This is the startup or beginning stage of most churches. This stage consists of a small, intimate and driven group of believers. This stage in the church life majority of the members are almost 100% committed and dedicated to the Sunday morning worship, Sunday evening service and even will come out to the Wednesday night Bible study. If the doors are open, they will be there.

2) Magnificent Stage. During this stage the church will reach a high level of attendance. Because of their size, money and growth the body begins to things that they could only dream of before. The problem is that during this stage and growth only about 50-65% of the church membership is in the committed group. They still have a vision and a dream but the depth and intensity of the potential begins to diminish.

3) Monument Stage. The church in this stage is still doing things to increase the growth, but they begin to talk less about the future than they do about their past. They start having to work harder at maintaining their successful past reputation. They do things because that's the way they have always done them…unfortunately this is what often brings the curse of power struggles and many members will begin to use the infamous language of "my church" that is the signal of the beginning of the end. The committed crowd now falls to about 15-30% of the congregation.

4) Mausoleum Stage. This is what is commonly called the "dead church." People have drifted away because of the lack of excitement and the baptistery hasn't been filled in several years with water because no one has given their heart to the Lord since the 1990's. The attendance levels of the stage fall to between 15-40% of the entire membership roster and when new people show up everyone turns around and stares wondering why.

Unfortunately the problem today is that there are far too many churches that stated off as churches, but aren't really churches any more. The sign still says they are a church and they still meet at a church building and sit in church pews and have all the materials that a real church uses, but they aren't a church anymore. Based on what they are doing and the results and impact that they are making on their community, they are nothing more than a social club. Rather than serving as a hospital for sinners, many churches have become a hotel for the saints.

What stage is your church in?

How can you tell if something is alive or dead? Well, in the physical body, a doctor would check for vital signs. The doctor would break out the stethoscope and listen for a heartbeat, grab your wrist and feel for a pulse, wrap you upper arm and check your blood pressure, or even in the old days pull a mirror out of his pocket and place in under the nose to see if you are breathing. But how about the vital signs of the church?

Here are a few things to check for:

GROWTH. Is the church growing? It is a sad state of the life of the church when they don't add one salvation during any given calendar year. This is the life pulse of the church to go and spread the Word of Christ to everyone. But to how no one receive Jesus as their Savior in any 12 month period....are you kidding? Face the facts. Death is just around the corner and it has your church in the crosshairs.

Let me make this clear, numerical growth isn't the only item that should be considered whether your church is alive or not but it is a bi-product of spreading the gospel of Jesus to the lost world!

But it should be an embarrassing equation when you have a big "goose egg" in the salvation column as the annual church report goes to print. This is true also in the individual Christian's life. Don't allow your pastor to be the only person that shares the prayer of salvation with a lost sinner. The great commission was declared to every believer not just pastors.

There should also be growth of the disciples that make up the body. Is the church producing bible reading and studying disciples of the Lord or is the growth only to a minimum. We need to continue to strive to wean our "baby" Christian off of the milk that they have been enjoying since the early 60's and start expecting them to chew a piece of meat or two of God's Word. The body should be growing in their prayer life, in their Bible study, in their evangelism. What about fasting? Oh no, not that! Ouch!

POWER. The problem with many churches today is that if the Holy Spirit would ever fall on them, it would be a total shock to the church congregation. We need to encourage the members, families and the children to believe in a Messiah that has the power to change their lives and make a miraculous difference in their families.

The church should still be the place where believers come to expect their sins to be forgiven and not broadcast all over the internet immediately following their revealing testimony. A place where habits can be broken, bondage can be loosened, and marriages can be healed. Not a place when repentance takes place at the altar during the invitation and every one wonders what the individual had done that brought them to their knees in the first place.

The church should still be the place where mercy and grace are freely given, relationships are repaired and forgiveness is granted. A place where unconditional love and acceptance is rampant for all attending not just granted to the ones that dress like us, look like us, believe like us and act like us. That is power.

These are just a few things that every church should possess to be a live, vibrant, God-fearing Body of Christ. When the Lord comes to receive His bride may he not find a house filled with zombies that are playing church but in reality have been residing in the graveyard experiencing death during each and every worship service.

WRITTEN IN STONE

A star on earth - a star in heaven
Karen Carpenter
located in Forest Lawn; Cypress, California

FINAL WORDS

My God. What's happened?
--Diana (Spencer), Princess of Wales, died August 31, 1997

CHAPTER 10
Church of the Living Dead

"Too many people are thinking of
security instead of opportunity.
They seem to be more afraid of life than death."
-James F. Bymes

I recently found an old bulletin clipart writing that was penned by an unknown author that lists several items regarding how to tell the difference between a living church and dead church. It goes like this:

1. Live churches welcome all who come through the door; Dead churches stick to their own kind!

2. Live church embers look for someone they can help. The members of a dead church look for something to complain about!

3. Live churches grow so fast that sometimes it's hard to keep up with people's names; in dead churches everybody always knows everybody's name.

4. Live churches may have some noisy children. Dead church are quiet as a cemetery.

5. Live churches keep changing their ways of doing things. Dead churches see no need for change!

6. Live churches support world missions. Dead churches keep the money at home!

7. Live churches sometimes spend more than their income. Dead churches don't need much money!

8. Live churches are full of regular, cheerful givers. Dead churches are full of grudging tippers!

9. Live churches spend a lot of time in prayer. Dead churches don't!

So what is the difference between a living church and a dead church? Simple. The difference is between religion and relationship. The difference is between head knowledge and heart knowledge. So literally, you can miss heaven by just twelve inches....the distance between your head and your heart.

When our lives have been touched by Jesus Christ, we want to tell others about it. There is a difference between life and death. When Jesus touches our lives as a church body, there are amazing changes and floods of life that flow into the entire congregation. There is a difference between life and death. When you have tasted the Glory of the Lord, you will never be satisfied again with the artificial feelings that they world tries to entice you with. There is a difference between life and death.

During the time of Alexander the Great there was a robber and murderer who went by the name of Alexander the Great as well. One day the famous ruler had the criminal brought in. He took a good long look at the man and then said, "What's your name?"

"Alexander the Great", the man answered.

"Is it true you've been lying, stealing and killing?"

"Yes"

With that the great leader looked at him, "You'd better change your name or change your ways."

The exact same is true with us as a church body. Those who know Jesus in their heart, those who have had a personal experience with Him need to continually show it to others both by what they say and by the way they act.

The perfect book of the Bible that should explain to us how to experience a true, relevant and living church is the book of Acts. I often wonder if we had no prior experience of the church of the last 200 years, if we had never heard of Baptists, Methodists, Catholics, or any of the other denominational families, and if we only had the knowledge of what the Book of Acts describes a church. How would we be different? I can't seem to find anything in my Bible about cookie cutter programs, rigid and dry bulletin led worship services or lifeless singing with people sitting in pews staring at the back of the heads of each other as we watch the "one-man show" each Sunday. We will look in-depth at what Acts tells us about the church in the next chapter.

We need to understand that the primary mission of the church today hasn't changed since Matthew 28:19 which says, "Therefore go and make disciples of all nations, baptizing them in the name of the Father and of the Son and of the Holy Spirit and teaching them to obey everything I have commanded you. And surely I am with you always, to the very end of the age." The mission of the church? To socialize? To demand that things go your way or no way? To complain about everyone that drops candy wrappers in the hymnal racks each Sunday? To moan about the length of the sermon or the way the preacher wears his hair? To show-off your newest dress? No! The church's mission is to make disciples.

What a shame that our church membership rolls are filled and jammed packed with names of people that haven't shadowed the door of "their" church in the past ten years. The Church of the Living Lord? I can almost hear the Lord whispering, "Either change your name or change your ways."

WRITTEN IN STONE

As the flowers are all made sweeter
by the sunshine and the dew,
so this old world is made brighter
by the lives
of folks like you.
Bonnie Parker
located in Crown Hill Cemetery; Dallas, Texas

FINAL WORDS

That was a great game of golf, fellers.
--Harry Lillis "Bing" Crosby, singer / actor, died October 14, 1977

CHAPTER 11
Deader Than a Doornail

"On a large enough time line, the survival rate for everyone will drop to zero."
-Chuck Palahniuk in Fight Club

The church has been classified as the only business that can go out of business and still stay in business for years. The church is also known for being similar to an axe without an axe head. It sure does make a lot of noise but doesn't get much done. How unfortunate!

The Apostle Paul had a great heart for the church. It was Paul who wrote in the book of Ephesians three things about the church of the Lord. He compared the church to:

1. A building. Reminding us of the foundation of the church.

2. A body. Reminding us of the function of the church.

3. A bride. Reminding us of the fidelity and love of the church.

Even though Paul loved the church he also took time to predict that there would come times of tragedy and days of difficulty for the church in the future. He said there would be times when men among them would speak perverse things, when people outside the flock would come as grievous wolves, seeking to devour the people of the Lord.

Look at Acts 20:28-32, *"Keep watch over yourselves and all the flock of which the Holy Spirit has made you overseers. Be shepherds of the church of God, which he bought with his own blood. I know that after I leave, savage wolves will come in among you and will not spare the flock. Even from your own number men will arise and distort the truth in order to draw away disciples after them. So be on your guard! Remember that for three years I never stopped warning each of you night and day with tears. Now I commit you to God and to the word of his grace, which can build you up and give you an inheritance among all those who are sanctified."*

I think the church is losing its power because of some of the tragedies that we have allowed to exist and grow in the church. For instance:

*The Unattended Church. Surveys tell us that almost 80% of the adult population of America is affiliated with someone's church or synagogue. But we find that only about 15-20% of these people can be found in church on any given Sunday.

The old saying goes "Sunday morning there is a blowout, Sunday night a little turnout and on Wednesday night a complete fallout." If we were to build the church on the average attendance of the mid-week Bible study service the majority of the churches would be the size of the pastor's office.

Hebrews 10:25 says, *"Let us not give up meeting together, as some are in the habit of doing, but let us encourage one another-and all the more as you see the Day approaching."*

*The Uncommitted People. It seems that this is one of the biggest problems in the church today, uncommitted people. We have a spectator church. It's like at a football stadium, you have 22 players that desperately need rest and 40,000 people in the stands that desperately need the exercise.

Where has all the commitment gone? The players are out there every day working, sweating and hitting their opponents just to get to a Super Bowl game. They have worked for it and deserve it. We, as Christians, go unprepared into battle daily, because we have been sitting in the bleachers far too long. The blessings are greater the closer you get to the field! The Sunday morning only, bored, uncommitted Christian just isn't going to make it victoriously in today's world.

*The Unbowed Knee. Our failure to pray. In the Book of Acts the faithful prayers of the 120 people in the upper room for ten days and on the day of Pentecost 3,000 souls were saved!

We have been given 1,440 minutes each day and how many of those minutes do we give back to the Lord in prayer? We need to spend much more time each day in intimate conversation with our Risen Lord. Prayer is the answer. When was the last time the alter of the church has been filled with Christians praying for the souls of lost people?

*The Unread Book. There is no doubt that we believe the Bible, but the tragedy is why do we not read it? If we aren't reading God's Word, there is no chance of us being where God wants us to be in our walk with Him.

*The Unconfessed Sin. We need to keep sin in our personal and private lives confessed to God on a daily basis. We cannot be used unhindered by God if we have sin in our hearts. I personally think that majority of the Christians of today's know very little about confession and repentance to our precious Lord and Savior. We must repent before the Lord can bring us back to life for Him.

*The Unexpressed Love. We don't show our love as much to each other and to God as we should. When is the last time you expressed your love to Him? God wants t hear that you love and care for Him. When is the last time you really laid bare your emotions before the Lord, and could say from the depths of your heart, that you really love and adore Jesus?

Do you that some people actually goes weeks or even months without hearing the words, "I love you?" When was the last time you told your family that you love them? Your wife or your husband? Your pastor or Sunday School teacher? Your friend or neighbor? We need to show our love to everyone, everyday.

WRITTEN IN STONE

Thank you for all the love you gave me.
There could be no one stronger.
Thank you for the many beautiful songs.
They will live long and longer.
Hank Williams
located in Oakwood Cemetery; Montgomery, Alabama

FINAL WORDS

That was the best ice-cream soda I ever tasted.
--Lou Costello, comedian, died March 3, 1959

CHAPTER 12
The unGrateful Dead

"Death and taxes are both certain...
but death isn't annual."
-Unknown

The idea of the church failing to live up to its potential isn't anything new. The book of Revelation deals with letters to the seven churches. But the one that seems to catch my eye is the church of Sardis.

This letter is found in Revelation 3:1-6. It says, *"To the angel of the church in Sardis write: These are the words of him who holds the seven spirits of God and the seven stars. I know your deeds; you have a reputation of being alive, but you are dead. Wake up! Strengthen what remains and is about to die, for I have not found your deeds complete in the sight of my God. Remember, therefore, what you have received and heard; obey it, and repent. But if you do not wake up, I will come like a thief, and you will not know at what time I will come to you. Yet you have a few people in Sardis who have not soiled their clothes. They will walk with me, dressed in white, for they are worthy. He who overcomes will, like them, be dressed in white. I will never blot out his name from the book of life, but will acknowledge his name before my Father and his angels. He who has an ear, let him hear what the Spirit says to the churches."*

First of all, I want to let you know that this church had a reputation. But the interesting thing about it is that the members of this congregation thought that their reputation was stellar. If you had asked members of the church of Sardis, "On a scale of 1 to 10, 10 being the best, where do you think your church stands with the Lord?" Every member probably would have answered a resounding, "10, of course!" They also would have added how alive and vibrant their church body was and how they are the envy of all the churches around.

As a matter of fact, the Bible even says that they had a "reputation of being alive" but in reality they were DEAD. They had all the meetings, programs, Bible studies, fellowships, and all the other "stuff" that churches do scheduled weekly. But they were DEAD. The activity of the church doesn't necessarily indicate the relationship the church has with the Lord. Sometimes churches are so busy that they don't have time to follow the lead of the Holy Spirit.

How sad that after the Lord evaluated this Sardis congregation, He indicated that their reputation wasn't quite what the members thought. He declared them "dead". The Lord doesn't really spend too much time here looking for flowery words to describe this body of believers. He goes straight to the heart of the matter without "candy coating" the facts. I personally think that every preacher should take note and start preaching in the same manner. Instead of speaking just to tickle the ears of the members, they should preach the fullness and boldness of God's Word each and every time they stand behind the pulpit.

The Devil was rejoicing that he had this church in his back pocket. I'm really not for sure that Satan wants every church in the United States today to worship him each Sunday morning. But I do think that the Devil would love to impact each church and "deaden" their members to where the body of believers have no significance on their community what so ever. He and his demons celebrate when the church becomes lifeless and mediocre.

The church in Sardis was not a threat. It wasn't changing lives. It wasn't witnessing. It wasn't anything except dead. What are some of the characteristics of a dead church? How can we recognize a dead church when we see one or when we are part of one?

Here are a few signs of a dead church:

*Lack of compassion. The parallels of a dead human body are similar to a dead church body. A dead person has not joy, no sadness, no happiness, no feelings. No compassion. The members of this church just didn't care about anything except themselves. When we stop having feelings toward each other you are on the way to certain death.

*Lack of warmth. A dead person's body temperature is cooler than the temperature of a living person. Cold. Indifferent. Loveless.

*Lack of movement. Obviously a dead body doesn't move. Neither does a dead church. If you aren't moving forward for the Lord then you are stagnant and working against Him.

Have you ever noticed at your favorite fast food restaurants that they are always adding something new to their menus? A chili, mushroom, bacon ranch hamburger with three quarter pound patties on an onion sprinkled bun, brushed with garlic butter and toasted over a hickory smoked grill. What? Who thinks of these things? Who buys these things? But take note at the next commercial and ask yourself, why? To keep things moving. To keep things new and alive.

The church should be exactly the same way. Don't expect your teenagers to beg to come to church every Sunday if your church soloist is singing

Pat Boone karaoke songs and listening to some minister delivering the message with no interest or excitement. I really believe that it is a critical sin to our Lord if we make church boring! We should have the most exciting and interesting services with new and vibrant ideas of how to bring the lost into our church each and every Sunday. How dare we allow people to sleep during church? No way!

If your pastor brings the same boring message with the same three points and a poem, in the same monotone voice each and every Sunday....give him and copy of this book and tell him to "move, man" or to pack your bags and really move, out of town. It's time that our ministers start responding to the excitement of the Word of God and stop worrying about their personal retirement plan and start preaching about our Risen Lord and Savior with the enthusiasm that Christ demands!

We will look at the prescription of how to resurrect the dead church back into the living church of God in the next chapter. Now put down this book and pray to the Lord that you get motivated and excited to put compassion, warmth and movement back into your relationship with your Lord and Savior.

WRITTEN IN STONE

Here Rests in
Honored Glory
An American
Soldier
Known But to God
Unknown Soldier
located in Arlington National Cemetery; Virginia

FINAL WORDS

I have a terrific headache.
--Franklin Delano Roosevelt, US President, died 1945

CHAPTER 13
Wake Up and Smell the Coffee

"When you are born, you cried and the world rejoiced.
Live your life so that when you die, the
world cries and you rejoice."
-Old Indian Proverb

We learned in the last chapter the characteristics of the dead church in Sardis. Now we are going to look at the declarations that God's Word tells us that we must do to come alive again.

Now let's shift gears and see what the letter to the Church of Sardis tells us about reviving what is left of a dead body. Christ makes it very clear that He has some important requirements that must be met to give your spiritual heart some much needed CPR.

1) Wake Up!

Jesus declares that the first thing a dead church or even a dead Christian needs to do is to "wake up" to the condition that you are in. This church thought that they had it all together. Scripture even mentioned that they "had a reputation that you are alive, but you are dead."

This was a wake up declaration to the entire church. Hey! Time to wake up and smell the coffee before it's too late. The sad issue in a lot of churches today that so many members of the congregation sleep through the service that they never give their heart, mind and spirit the time to hear the message from the Lord.

Today a wake up call comes in many different ways. My personal wake up message came loud and clear when I was 19 years old and was involved in a head-on collision going around 60 miles an hour. As I lay in the hospital bed that evening there was no doubt the Jesus whispered in my ear but screamed in my heart. He opened my spiritually sleep-matted eyes and told me to "wake up or I will take away from you what I've so freely gave." He wasn't threatening to take away my salvation, He was saying either use the talent I've given you for my glory or it will be taken away.

That evening I rededicated my walk with the Lord and received a confirmation from Him that He will keep His word forever. A spiritual wake up call.

This letter makes it clear that now is the time to come alive for Jesus. The book of Romans declares, "*Wake up for the time of our salvation is nearer now than when we first believed. This is not a time to be spiritually asleep.*"

2) Remember Up!

Revelation 3:3 says, "Remember, therefore, what you have received and heard and obey it." If it's true that some people have spiritual sleeping sickness, there are also some Christians who are afflicted with spiritual amnesia. They have forgotten what God has done for them in the past. Some have become apathetic but we need to remember there has never been a time when God has ever failed us.

I remember that very day that I received Jesus Christ as my Lord and Savior. I was only 7 years old, but the day in my mind and heart was like yesterday. It was during a Sunday evening service and I vividly remember how the Spirit was convicting me and leading me to ask Jesus to be my Savior. Do you remember where you were when you were saved? Was it at church, during a revival, or a church camp, or Vacation Bible School? When was it that you first came to know the Lord? Doesn't it do something in your heart to remember the way it was?

That's what Jesus is saying if you are dead, just go back in your mind and remember how it used to be and do those things again that you were doing then. Do you remember how excited you were about Jesus? You need to recapture that excitement. Remember your salvation.

3) Repent Up!

Now look at the last part of Revelation 3:3 it says, *"Remember, therefore, what you have received and heard; obey it and repent!"* He goes on to say, *"If you don't wake up, I'm going to come like a thief."* He is simply saying, "Repent." Why? Because Jesus Christ could come back at any moment.

1 John 2:28 says, *"And now, little children, abide in Him so that when He shall appear we'll have the confidence before Him and not be ashamed at His coming."* Basically, He is saying to get your life right with the Lord now, before I come again. Evaluate your habits, your lifestyle and repent.

There are so many things that clog our spiritual pipeline to a free-flowing relationship with God. If your life isn't flowing the way it should maybe it's time to clear the debris out of our lives. Could it be a bad habit or lousy attitude? Clean them out and repent. Then once again the flow will begin and there will be power in your life again. Proverbs 28:3 says, *"Whoever covers their sins shall not prosper, but whoever confesses and forsakes them shall have mercy."* Don't cover them up with God. Repent of it.

WRITTEN IN STONE

Chief of the Hunkpapa Sioux
Sitting Bull
located in Post Cemetery; Fort Yates, North Dakota

FINAL WORDS

They couldn't hit an elephant at this dist. . . .
(He was killed in battle during the US Civil War)
--General John Sedgwick, Union Commander, died 1864

CHAPTER 14
Dead Silence

"Some people are so afraid to die that they never begin to live."
-Henry Van Dyke

REFLECTION AND REVIEW DAY:

By now you know the routine. Go ahead and pour a nice cup of coffee, turn the TV off, find a quiet secluded place, grab your Bible and spend some quality time sitting at the feet of Jesus and soaking in what He has to say to you. This should be a time to grow and write down your thoughts on each of this week's chapters. So pray for wisdom, guidance and insight. Take a sip of coffee and a gulp of the Spirit and let's go!

Chapter 8: The First Community Church of the Comatose"

*Honestly evaluate you church and ministries. Vibrant? Alive? Coma-bound?

___

___

___

___

*What's the image that your Church Body is reflecting in your community?

___

___

___

___

*On a scale of 1 to 10, is your pastor/pastors exhibiting "life" from the pulpit or is the sermons more like a funeral service.

___

___

___

Chapter 9: House of 1,000 Corpses"

*What stage is your church at right now: Movement, Magnificent, Monument, Mausoleum?

*What about the GROWTH at your church?

*How is the POWER being utilized?

Chapter 10: "Church of the Living Dead"

*Describe the signs of a Religion based church.

____

____

____

____

*Now how about the Relationship vital signs that you notice in your church body.

____

____

____

____

*What is the overall mission of your church?

____

____

____

Chapter 11: Deader Than a Doornail"

*Evaluate the Six "Uns":

-Unattended Church

-Uncommitted People

-Unbowed Knee

-Unread Book

-Unconfessed Sin

-Unexpressed Love

Chapter 12: The unGrateful Dead

*Reread the Revelation 3:1-6. Are there any characteristics that are described in the Sardis church that would parallel the characteristics at yours?

____

____

____

____

*Does your church keep the Devil on the run or does the Devil run your church?

____

____

____

*Think about the signs of a dead church: lack of compassion, lack of warmth and lack of movement. Are any of these signs "hanging" around your church?

____

____

____

Chapter 13: **Wake Up and Smell the Coffee**"

*What are some of the things that need to experience a spiritual "wake up" call?

____

____

____

____

*Take time right now to write a few things that you as an individual and as a church body need to remember about His presence in your life.

____

____

____

____

*List some of the miracles that the Lord has performed in your life and in the life of your local church.

____

____

*Repent. Ouch! But spend a few moments and try to experience pure repentance in your walk with Christ.

*What are a few items that your church should repent for that could be considered direct sins against the Lord. They could be sins of commission (things that have been done wrong) or sins of omission (things that should have been done but weren't).

WRITTEN IN STONE

I never met a man I didn't like.
Will Rogers
located in Will Rogers Memorial; Claremore, Oklahoma

FINAL WORDS

Here am I, dying of a hundred good symptoms.
--Alexander Pope, writer, died May 30, 1744

CHAPTER 15
Dead Man Walking

"God pours life into death and death into life without a drop being spilled."
-Author Unknown

Back to when I was 19 years old and having the automobile accident that redirected my life forever. I became a Christian when I was 7 years old, called to preach when I was 12 years old, but when I was 19...I was doing everything on my own. However, after being born again there was a lot of growing and maturing that needed to take place in my life. Rather than living by faith I found myself at times trying to be the person God wanted me to be on my own. And the harder I tried the more I seemed to fail and fall short. I'm getting ahead of myself here a little bit but I want to share with you a verse that may just "change your life" because what Paul wrote to the Galatians could well have been written of me and you.

The New Living Translation of Galatians 3:3 says, *"Have you lost your senses? After starting your Christian lives in the Spirit, why are you now trying to become perfect by your own human effort?"*

I love how that verse puts it. "Have you lost your senses?" "Have you lost your mind?" "What are you thinking?" If you couldn't save yourself why do you think you can sanctify yourself? All I knew was this: even though I was a Christian I still felt and knew that there must be something more. No matter how hard I tried to live up to God's standards and do the right thing that I knew to do, I just kept falling short. There had to be more and there was something more, but I was guilty of trying to get in on my own.

If you have ever or do now feel that way, then this chapter is for you. The chapter title, "Dead Man Walking" speaks to the verse that Paul pens in Galatians 2:20a, *"I am crucified with Christ; nevertheless I live."*

A couple of thoughts about life: It is a matter of being, not behaving! It is a matter of faith, not feeling!

On the one hand Paul had died with Christ and on the other hand he was still living. Paul was literally a dead man walking. We are going to dive into the second chapter of Galatians and discover how to experience that "something more" in our lives. Before we jump in, let's set the stage.

Here's a little history and background. While Paul was ministering in Antioch, Peter came for a visit and Paul ended up having to confront Peter to his face in front of the people. Why? Because when Peter first came to Antioch he was associating with the Gentile Christians there. He would even eat his meals with them going so far as to eat pork which was something that was strictly forbidden from the Jewish diet, but Christ had now declared it ok to eat. So everything was going smoothly. But then some Jewish Christians came along who believed that the only way to be saved was to trust in Christ and follow the Old Testament rules and regulations of the Jewish law. When they came to town Peter stopped eating ham sandwiches and even worse he stopped associating with the Gentile Christians. To make matters worse he was influencing other Christian leaders like Barnabas to do the same thing.

So Paul confronted him to his face in front of everyone and basically accused him of being hypocritical. He reminded Peter that people are saved through faith in Jesus Christ and not through keeping Jewish rituals. He basically told Peter that he was sending conflicting messages by on the one hand holding to these outdated regulations. The example that he was setting didn't match the message that he was teaching.

This is what was at stake here. If one is saved by faith alone, do you then need to maintain and advance in your walk with the Lord by keeping certain rules and regulations? Or do you continue on by faith as well. It is by faith that we are saved and it is by faith that we grow in grace and it is by faith that we are sanctified.

There is no exact equivalent in our modern way of life with the Jewish laws referred to here. They had rules about how many times they washed their hands, what kinds of meat they could eat and how far they could walk on Saturdays. But we can and do get into our legalistic ways of thinking some times.

Imagine if someone from another denomination walked into your church and said, "The people in this church aren't real Christians and this is not a real church. You don't have stained glass windows or a pipe organ. Your pastor doesn't wear a robe or a clerical collar. Therefore you are not a real church."

Now you know in your heart that this just isn't true. You know that those things don't make a church a church. Those are external things not eternal things. Peter was guilty of emphasizing external things over eternal things and Paul was going to set him straight. Paul basically told Peter that he was leading people astray by living out a religion of externals and that there was more to it than that. Then Paul goes on to describe that "something more."

I want you to see that advancing in the Christian life is not about rituals and regulations and rules. It is about a relationship with Jesus Christ—a life-long, life-changing relationship.

There is only one way to experience that "something more" in your life. You have to die. Not physically of course, but internally. That is why this chapter is called, "Dead Man Walking." You have to be crucified with Christ. Here are a few truths that will help you to experience that "something more" in your personal life today.

Life is indeed a valuable commodity and all of us want to be alive, but we really want more than that, BUT being alive is one thing, really living is another!

Did you know that not everyone who is alive really lives?

In fact, everywhere you go, you encounter people who are desperately attempting to really live. They are actually trying to answer a basic question right out of philosophy 101-"What is the meaning of life?"

*Many determine that the meaning of life is to be found in material possessions, so they set themselves to acquire them.

*Others determine that the meaning of life is to be found in pleasure, so they set out to indulge themselves.

*Still others determine that the meaning of life is to be found in career, money, or social standing. They become workaholics, greedy, and class conscious and the thing that all these groups have in common, is a relentless and desperate, even frantic pursuit of these things.

The sad reality is, even when they attain a measure of these things, they find that they are still unfulfilled.

We Christians want to really live, too, don't we? Most of us have answered the question: "What is the meaning of life?" At least intellectually, if not theologically.

What we really want to know is: "What is the meaning of life, specifically for me?" How does it impact me? How do I live "in Christ?" We don't want to know how to merely exist as a Christian, we want to know how to REALLY LIVE as a Christian!

We want to kick up our heels and watch the money flow into our bank accounts and we want to order God around like He is our Servant or Sugar Daddy! Well, I hate to disappoint those who believe such nonsense, but, God is nobody's Sugar Daddy in spite of what your favorite televangelist tells you.

Life is hard, at best, and we get terminally ill, fired, laid off, have financial reversals, face rejection, divorce and the list is endless. Those unhappy events are allowed to invade our "happy lives" to get us into position for God to: use us, teach us, correct us, discipline us and yes, bless us.

In the Bible, there are some foundational truths from which Christians should never stray and yet we spend more time reading a book by Dr. Phil than we do the Word of God and we run into one of the "problems" of life and we are crushed! We don't know what to do because Dr. Phil's formula for success didn't work for you.

In Galatians 2:20, we find the answer to the questions we have about life and we find the secret of how to really live. The truth of Galatians 2:20 is that real spiritual life comes from death and in order to be truly alive, we have to understand that we are truly dead.

It is one of the greatest paradoxes in all of scripture. It's the mystery of the Kingdom. Jesus said, "We must lose our lives in order to find them." He also said that if we seek to hold on to our lives we will lose them.

Now, Paul is saying here in Galatians 2:20, that though we are dead, we really live, but how can these things be?

1) We need a new provision of life.

We're not the only ones who struggle with living for Jesus, Christians everywhere struggle and they always have and that struggle comes from our desire to be in Christ, and our realization that we are powerless to live for Him. That sometimes leaves us frustrated and we give up on becoming a spiritually mature believer.

The streets and lanes of our community are littered with spiritually dead and dying Christians who gave up, got their little feelings hurt, didn't get their named called or got their named called to serve and they got mad about it and quit or raised such a stink you could smell it all the way in Chicago.

Listen to me; do you honestly sense the longing for the Lord's life and the recognition of the powerlessness to attain it? This should be the cry of every believer's heart: "Lord, take charge. Divorce me from my enemy. Imprison me. Make me Your own."

The good news is that God has not only anticipated that need but made a way for us. Our God, at the moment we were born again, gave us a new provision of life and He tells us that this life only comes out of the death of our own personal ambitions, desires and priorities!

Am I there yet? No sir, but I work on it every day because I am getting closer to sunset than I am sunup, if you get my drift? The key to the spirit filled life, understanding and accepting that the old me, with all my limitations and problems, need to be put to death. Paul says, "I have been crucified with Christ."

This is really important; God doesn't want perfection out of you, He wants Holiness which translated in both Hebrew and Greek means: Maturity. This is the first thing we must understand. It is a key to understanding who we really are, now that we are in Christ.

It is a key to releasing us from the struggle of trying to live the Christian life by our own strength and power. Perfection is more than we can do, and it is more than we have been asked to do.

You can clean up the old self, perfume it, put new clothes on it, educate it, and otherwise seek to improve it, but all you have is still the old self. But what we need is not the old self, we need a new self. And in order for the new self to come forth, the old self must be dealt with and the way God has chosen to deal with the old self is not to reform it, but to remove it. This is what it means "to be crucified with Christ." We are now under no obligation to the old life, because we have been set free from it. We are dead to our old way of living. Sin no longer has any control over us.

Satan no longer has any right to us. We are no longer who we were. We are crucified with Christ, so that God could give us a new life.

Paul says, *"I have been crucified with Christ; and it is no longer I who live, but Christ lives in me."* I'm dead, yet alive!

*This is what God has done for us.

*Out of death comes life, but it is not our life.

*It is the life of Jesus Christ being lived in us.

*Someone has called this the exchanged life.

*We exchange our life for His. What a deal!

Now, before we close this chapter (and we will conclude this look at Galatians 2:20-21 in the next chapter) we can quit struggling to live by our own strength and begin to learn how to depend on His life in us. Does that make sense?

This is what Paul meant in Philippians 1:21, when he said, "*For to me, to live is Christ.*" In other words, the meaning of life for Paul was that Jesus Christ was now in his life, living His life in him (Paul).

Let me explain it like this: A glove cannot do anything by itself. It needs a hand to fill it, but when the glove has a hand inside like Ty Pennington, of Extreme Makeover, it can fix anything.

We Christians are like gloves. What we need is the Lord to fill us with His power and then we will be able to do all things through Christ, who is living in us. That is precisely what we have now in Christ.

Colossians 2:9-10 says, *"For in Him all the fullness of deity dwells in bodily form, and in Him you have been made complete."*

The only way to be able to experience the life that Christ wants to live through you is to "die" to self and "live" for Him. Become a "dead man walking." Get it?

WRITTEN IN STONE

1880 - 1946
W.C. Fields
located in Forest Lawn; Glendale, California

FINAL WORDS

There is no God but Allah and Muhammad is God's messenger.
(He was executed by hanging, at Camp Justice
in the Baghdad suburb of Khadimiya)
--Saddam Hussein died December 30, 2006

CHAPTER 16
Dead Man Walking, Part 2

"The fear of death flows from the fear of life.
A man who lives fully is prepared to die at any time."
-Mark Twain

As we continue to look at Galatians 2:20-21, we learned in the last chapter that:

1) We Need a New Provision of Life.

Now we will look at the second item these scriptures bring to light.

2) We Need a New Perspective of Living.

I want to reveal to you the way my crazy mind works. For the past several weeks I couldn't stop thinking about this reality. Are you ready? Here it goes: It has come to my attention that it is possible for a rat to live his entire life in a barn and never become a horse. What? Think about it. This is deep.

It is also possible for a Christian to live his entire life in possession of the truth of who he is, and never walk in it.

*What we need are eyes to see who we are in Christ.

*What we need is faith to believe and walk in that truth, and that is what God has given us.

*There are some people, books, music, movies, sermons, events that when we are impacted by them, leave us never the same.

I recently read a true story in a mission magazine written by an American Indian who was also a missionary about an Apache Chief who said: "There came to our tribe a man and he extolled the God of the white-man. We told him to leave and there came another man and he said: 'do not drink anymore fire-water, do not get drunk, and do not steal.' We paid no attention to him. Then there came a man who told us about a God who came down from heaven to live among us, who so loved us that He shared our life and died in our place for our sins, and who opened the doors whereby we might be saved and enter heaven. 'We never forget that.'"

You see, what is true about us is only received by us through a revelation of that truth when you were saved.

*Were you saved when you received it and when you realized that Christ died for you?

*When did He die for you? He died for you 2,000 years ago, but when did you appropriate it?

*Did you appropriate it when you saw the truth of it and began to act on it. I did and I was just 7 years old.

*It was a revelation of God to me and it was a revelation of God to those of you that have been saved, and you and I have never been the same!

When we begin to expect the Lord to live in us and through us, our lives will begin to reach the potential God has always planned for us. Expectations are very powerful and they mean so much to us don't they? Even the expectations of others toward us make a difference.

Did you ever see the Oscar winning movie entitled: "Stand and Deliver?" It is the true story of a math teacher named Jaime Escalante and played by the brilliant James Olmos, who taught at Garfield High School in East Los Angeles, a tough, poor Hispanic neighborhood.

The school was being overrun with gang violence, but he took a group of 18 unmotivated students, many of whom would have never graduated from high school, and convinced them to take advanced placement calculus, when most some of them struggled with basic addition. Most of the students hated school, but this quite non-assuming man motivated these students by going to where they lived.

In one scene, the teacher walked by a kid working on a carburetor and he said, "You know, someday you could be designing those things instead of repairing them." His love for those kids was constant and persistent. Throughout the movie his constant word of praise was, "you're the best!" and they began to believe it.

For most of those kids, it was the first time anyone had believed in them, in fact. He got them to commit themselves to stay after school every day from 3-5 pm, and come in on Saturday morning to prepare for the national advanced placement exam in calculus.

When the test results came back, it was staggering, because all 18 students had passed. Never had so many students from one school passed the test, in the state of California. In fact, the test service didn't believe it, and accused the student of cheating. So six months later, Jaime Escalante convinced the students to take the test again and all 18 passed the second time.

The results have continued to multiply each and every year and each year over 100 students from Garfield High School pass the exam. Expectations are powerful instruments in our lives and in the lives of our children.

3) We Need a New Perspective on How God Sees Us.

Let me share another true story that has been floating around on the internet for years. The story is about Teddy Stallard, who by his own admission was an unattractive, unmotivated little boy, difficult to like, especially for a school teach who all day long faced his expressionless, unfocused stare.

Although his fifth grade teacher said she loved all her students, Miss Thompson had to admit that deep down she wasn't being honest. She didn't like the kid, and she enjoyed a certain perverse pleasure in marking his papers with "F"s with flair. Her view of him was already distorted by her perspective, but she should have known better.

As his teacher, she had his records, and she knew more about him than she wanted to admit.

*First grade: Teddy shows promise with his work and attitude, but he has a poor home situation.

*Second grade: Teddy could do better. Mother is seriously ill. He receives little help at home.

*Third grade: Teddy is a good boy, but too serious. He is a slow learner. His mother died this year.

*Fourth grade: Teddy is very slow but well behaved. His father shows no interest.

At Christmas, her class all brought her presents in pretty wrappings, and gathered round to watch her open them. She was surprised when she received a gift from Teddy. It was crudely wrapped in brown paper, loosely held together with tape. When she opened it, out fell a gaudy rhinestone bracelet with half the rhinestones missing, and a bottle of cheap perfume.

The children began to giggle, but she had enough sense to put on the bracelet and apply some of the perfume on her wrist and she asked the class, "doesn't it smell lovely?" When school was over and the children had left, Teddy lingered behind and slowly came over to her desk and said softly, "Miss Thompson, you smell just like my mother. Her bracelet looks really pretty on you, too. I'm glad you like my presents."

When Teddy left, Miss Thompson got down on her knees and asked God to forgive her.

The next day when the children came to school, they were welcomed by a new teacher. Miss Thompson had become a new person.

She was no longer just a teacher; she had become an agent of God. She was now a person committed to loving her children and doing things for them that would live on after her. By the end of that school year,

Teddy showed dramatic improvement and had caught up with most of the students.

She didn't hear from Teddy for a long time and then one day she received a note that said, "Dear Miss Thompson: I wanted you to be the first to know. I will be graduating second in my class. Love, Teddy Stallard."

Four years later, she received another note: "Dear Miss Thompson: They just told me I will be graduating first in my class. I wanted you to be the first to know. The university had not been easy, but I like it. Love, Teddy Stallard."

A few years later, she received another note: "Dear Miss Thompson: As of today I am Theodore Stallard, M.D. how about that? I wanted you to be the first to know. I am getting married next month, the 27th and I want you to come and sit where my mother would sit if she were alive. You are the only family I have now, dad died last year. Love, Teddy Stallard."

Miss Thompson went to that wedding and she sat where Teddy's mother would have sat; she had earned that right. She had done something for Teddy that he could never forget.

How others see us is important, but how God sees us is essential and how we see ourselves is vital. If we can see ourselves for who we really are, with Christ living his life through us, we will never be the same. The presence of Christ changes everything. We are alive in Him and because of that we can say with Paul, "The life which I now live in the flesh I live by faith in the son of God, who loved me, and delivered Himself up for me."

That is the truth about who we are from God's perspective-we are not who we once were, because the living Lord resides in us and we contain the living Lord, who is our life! Now that's REAL living!

WRITTEN IN STONE

"That's All Folks!"
The Man of a Thousand Voices
Mel Blanc
located in Hollywood Memorial Park; Hollywood, California

FINAL WORDS

This is the last of earth! I am content.
--John Quincy Adams, US President,
died February 21, 1848

CHAPTER 17
Dead Poets Society

"Because I have loved life, I shall have no sorrow to die."
-Amelia Burr

I used to love to play golf. I haven't played the game in years, but one thing that I vividly remember is a rule that applies to golf and now that I think about it, playing the fiddle. The rule is this: You have to practice really hard just to be considered "bad".

That reminds me of a famous golf story. A Scotsman was demonstrating the game of golf to U.S. President Ulysses S. Grant. With a gallery of newspaper reporters watching, the Scotsman carefully placed the golf ball on a tee, positioned himself in the correct golfing stance, and then took a mighty swing. The club hit the turf and scattered dirt all over the President's beard and the crowd with him. When the dust settled, the golf ball was still sitting untouched on the tee. Once again the Scotsman swung and again he missed. After several more attempts and misses, finally the Scotsman stopped. President Grant waited patiently, wiped dirt from his face and beard and said, "There seems to be a fair amount of exercise in the game, but I fail to see the purpose of the ball."

President Grant's statement that could be so true to many of us today, there's a lot of activity going on today, but is there life? Is there purpose?

What's the point of it all? We have so many things that connect us to so many people today. Just think: The Internet. I can sit in my living room and instant message someone across town or on the other side of the world. Cell phones. You can speak to anybody, anytime, anywhere. Now we have blackberries. I can e-mail, read the world news, take photographs and talk on the cell phone…all at the SAME TIME. But the key question is: Is there any purpose in all of this activity? Where is the life?

Many people have all the activity around them every day, but still feel empty, alone, lifeless. Their happiness, excitement and purpose depend largely on mere circumstance and achievements. Life surrounding them but they are not experiencing it. Empty. Dead.

The Bible shows us how to transfer our dead lives to a vibrant life of extreme fullness. This emptiness isn't anything new, Paul in the book of Colossians addresses this very problem when he wrote to a group of Christians who were dealing with the problem of finding meaning, purpose and life in their lives.

Colossians 1:9-12 *"For this reason, since the day we heard about you, we have not stopped praying for you and asking God to fill you with the knowledge of his will through all spiritual wisdom and understanding. And we pray this in order that you may live a life worthy of the Lord and may please him in every way: bearing fruit in every good work, growing in the knowledge of God, being strengthened with all power according to his glorious might so that you may have great endurance and patience, and joyfully giving thanks to the Father, who has qualified you to share in the inheritance of the saints in the kingdom of light."*

Paul mentions three areas of life that he is praying for the believers in the above scripture. First, Paul's prayer was a request for the continued growth of these Christians in the spite of all the heresies and lifelessness of the false teachers around them. He is asking for:

1) Filled Living. Notice the word "filled" in verse 9, "asking God to fill you." Filled with what? Filled with the knowledge of the Lord's will, the purpose that He has already destined to be in our lives. Spiritual wisdom and understanding should be sought from the Lord so we can fully live the empowered life that Christ has blueprinted for us before we were ever even born.

To be fully alive and successful in life we must seek, find and follow God's will. So what is God's will for your life? There are two ways to look at it; first of all, in the general sense God's will is that all people come to the knowledge and salvation of the Lord. But then the Lord's will gets really specific.

God has a specific purpose, will and direction for each of us to fulfill in our lives. It is not by chance. So how do I find it? Use the three guides that the Lord provides to each of us. The Bible, The Holy Spirit and Godly Direction from friends in your life are your "green lights" to life. Before proceeding make sure these three lines up and then you can be fairly certain that you are on the right course headed for Christ's perfect will in your life.

2) Fruitful Living. To experience living a life to the fullest means to daily produce fruit in your Christian walk. To be able to produce fruit in our lives it is essential that our branch is attached to the vine of Christ or our fruit will never be developed properly. This is the reason that there is so much "bad apples and sour grapes" in church. The fruit in your life can only receive the proper nutrition which is adequate food and water. Jesus in the Bread of Life and Jesus is the Water of Life. In John 15 Jesus taught us that He is the vine and we are the branches.

The branch's job is to stay completely attached to the vine, and then the fruit will be flowing throughout our lives.

A good test to see if you are living life to the fullest is to check with Galatians 5:22-23 and go down the check list of spiritual fruit, *"The fruit of the Spirit is love, joy, peace, patience, kindness, goodness, faithfulness, and self-control. Against such things there is no law."*

3) Powerful Living. One of my favorite movies of all time is "Dead Poets Society". Robin Williams portrays an instructor in a private and elite school for young men. One of the best scenes of the movie is where Williams' character brings the entire class to the trophy room of the school. There they see photos and faces of so many past graduates. The instructor asks the students to "huddled up," lean in and listen then he whispers those famous words, "Carpe Diem".

"Seize the day." Don't let the power of the possibility to make an impact on your life or someone else's life, pass you by.

So many people in America have the wrong idea of what powerful and successful lives really are. True success is being exactly in the middle of what God has in store just for you. True living is experiencing the fullness of Christ in your life each and every day. Seize the day and watch Jesus' power explode from your life onto others making life changing impact.

Anything less just isn't true living. Will Rogers said is best, "So live that you would not mind selling your pet parrot to the town gossip."

4) Joyful Living. John 15:11 says, *"I have told you these things that my joy may remain in you and that your joy may be full."* In Colossians 1:12 it continues, *"joyfully giving thanks to the Father who has qualified you to share in the inheritance of the saints."* To be joyful you must be thankful.

Self-center people are never grateful; they feel that they deserve the things that they are getting. A joyful life consists of praising God and thanking the others around you.

Our joy isn't supposed to be demolished by either difficult circumstances or difficult people. The source of our joy is God. It is a limitless source. A source that never runs dry. Dry Christians have moved away from the well, not the well from the Christians.

How alive are you with your walk with the Lord? Remember, He hasn't moved and He is waiting and willing to bring the fullness of your destiny to life today.

SSSSHHHHHH……

Huddle up.

Listen.

"Carpe Diem, Seize the day!"

WRITTEN IN STONE

She did it the hard way.
Bette Davis
located in Forest Lawn; Hollywood Hills, California

FINAL WORDS

How were the receipts today at Madison Square Garden?
--P. T. Barnum, entrepreneur, died 1891

CHAPTER 18
The Final Interment?

"I am ready to meet my Maker. Whether my Maker
Is prepared for the great ordeal of
meeting me is another matter."
-Winston Churchill

Mark 10:46-52 says, *"Then they came to Jericho . As Jesus and his disciples, together with a large crowd, were leaving the city, a blind man, Bartimaeus (that is, the Son of Timaeus), was sitting by the roadside begging. When he heard that it was Jesus of Nazareth, he began to shout, "Jesus, Son of David, have mercy on me!" Many rebuked him and told him to be quiet, but he shouted all the more, "Son of David, have mercy on me!" Jesus stopped and said, "Call him." So they called to the blind man, "Cheer up! On your feet! He's calling you." Throwing his cloak aside, he jumped to his feet and came to Jesus. "What do you want me to do for you?" Jesus asked him. The blind man said, "Rabbi, I want to see." "Go," said Jesus, "your faith has healed you." Immediately he received his sight and followed Jesus along the road".*

How predictable is your life? Do you do the same thing day after day after day after day? Are you just going through the motions without experiencing the "life" that should be included? The above scripture gives us seven great principals to apply to our "mundane" life to break it wide open with newness.

Have you ever been stuck in a rut? You've heard that a rut is a grave with both ends knocked out.

I grew up in the country in Southern Illinois where ruts were a regular part of life. When it rained all the side dirt roads turned to mud. The first person to go down one of those roads created ruts to wherever they were going. If you happen to turn onto the road with ruts, you went where the ruts went. Many times as a young boy I found myself stuck in the ruts going somewhere that I didn't want to go. Many times the only way to get out of the ruts was for someone to come and pull you out. If you had to drive down the road with ruts you had to make sure that you never let your wheels slip into the ruts.

There are times in all of our lives that we get into the ruts. When we say someone is "in a rut" or that they are "stuck in a rut," we mean that the person is locked into a behavior that, like that road, they're stuck in the ruts that aren't easily escaped.

A rut can be a certain pattern of behavior that we are locked into that we don't like. Some ruts are bad because they keep us locked into a lifestyle that is destructive. Some ruts keep us from making progress in our lives. They keep us from growing and becoming all that God wants us to be. There are some ruts that we all need to avoid. The rut of a prayer-less life, the rut of missing church, the rut of not reading God's Word and the rut of not paying tithes.

Some ruts are good, habitual behavior that captivates us and helps us grow and develop. But more often than not, when we say we're stuck in a rut, we mean that we're having difficulty escaping a wrong behavior.

Probably all of us, at one time or another, get the wheels of our lives stuck in ruts, so the main question is: How do you go about breaking out of a rut?

In the above scripture we find Bartimaeus who was a blind beggar who lived in the ancient city of Jericho. It wouldn't be a far stretch of the imagination to say that he was probably stuck in some ruts. Blind Bartimaeus made his living by begging. But Bartimaeus was tired of living in the ruts, tired of begging, tired of being pitied and he was going to break out of the ruts that kept him from becoming all that he could be.

But Bartimaeus got out! There are at least seven things Bartimaeus did that day when Jesus passed by his begging position that helped get him out of his rut. The actions Bartimaeus took that day suggest seven things you and I can do when we find ourselves in a rut.

The first principal is:

1) Assume Responsibility For Your Own Life.

Mark 10: 47 says, *"And when he heard that it was Jesus the Nazarene, he began to cry out and say, "Jesus, Son of David, have mercy on me!"*

Notice here that Bartimaeus took the initiative himself to cry out. That is a very important observation, perhaps the most important of all the seven principals.

Do you remember the days of your childhood when, if you were uncomfortable, or afraid, or hurting, you would cry out for Mom and she would come to your rescue? They would comfort you and say, 'don't be afraid, I'll take care of you."

Then came the time in your life when you left home, an action that could have been at first, a little scary. Could you make it on your own? Would you have to go back to Mom and Dad in humiliation?

Most people do a lot of growing up in those first couple of years on their own. Maybe the best definition there is to describe someone who is "grown up" is someone who has assumed responsibility for his or her own life.

One of the main reasons it is so hard to break out of a rut is because it is so secure sometimes in the rut! It is safe. It gets really comfortable in there. The rut becomes a way of life for us. It's familiar and gives us security, but it's a false sense of security.

Think for a moment about whatever rut you may be in. You can continue to blame your parents, or society, or your nationality, or your abuse, or your rotten luck, or your lack of self discipline, or the "fat" genes you inherited from your parents, or whatever. You're certainly free to do so but there is a price for that dubious "freedom." You'll be a rut dweller for the rest of your entire life. You might as well quit dreaming. Leave out all the hope. Quit thinking about the day when your ship will finally come in or someone will reach down and pull you out. Getting out of those ruts is only for those who refuse to make excuses and start assuming responsibility for themselves.

2) Believe You Can Change

For Bartimaeus, it took some real faith that day to cast aside his jacket, jump up, and move in the direction of the sound of the crowd surrounding Jesus. Verse 52 says, *"God your way; your faith has made you well."*

Where does that faith come from, anyway? Are we talking about a kind of hopeful "leap in the dark" when we talk of believing you can change? I don't think so. Faith must be based on some evidence; otherwise it is nothing more than gullibility. Notice that phrase in verse 47, "And when he heard that it was Jesus the Nazarene, he began to cry out."

That implies some recognition. Some prior knowledge. Bartimaeus had probably heard how Jesus had healed others.

How does that apply to you and me? The Bible says in Romans 10:17, *"So faith comes from hearing, and hearing by the Word of Christ."* Hearing such stories produces faith and this is one of the greatest uses of the Bible.

In the real world most people don't believe people can change. They're busy perfecting the art of blaming others and explaining why change is impossible. They've made so many excuses for themselves and others that anything beyond mediocrity now sounds impossible.

There is sufficient evidence both in the Bible and in experience to assure you that you can break out of your rut. But you must convince yourself by believing you can change.

3) Clarify What You Really Need

Notice in verse 51 what Jesus asked Bartimaeus, "What do you want Me to do for you?"

Why did Jesus ask that? Was He blind? Couldn't He just read the man's mind? Didn't He already know? Here is an important point; Jesus asked the question for Bartimaeus' benefit. It was asked for Bartimaeus and those who were watching.

We seldom do anything about the ruts we live in until circumstances force us into our awareness. Even then, we seldom move until we finally get to the place where we set a goal.

A life with no goals is a life of a rut dweller. If you have no goals, quit dreaming. Your chance of hitting something you don't aim for is virtually impossible. Certainly if you hope to break out of a rut, you have to be willing to clarify what it is you really need and want.

"What do you want Me to do for you?" Jesus asked. Bartimaeus didn't hesitate: "Rabboni, I want to regain my sight!"

4) Stop Worrying About What Other People Will Say

Verse 48 says, *"And many were sternly telling him to be quiet, but he kept crying out all the more, "Son of David, have mercy on me!"*

One major hurdle that keeps many of us in our ruts is the fear of disapproval or rejection from others.

Bartimaeus didn't have to image what others would say if he stepped forward that day. They told him, "And many were sternly telling him to be quiet." "Shut up, Bartimaeus! Jesus isn't interested in people like you!"

You see Bartimaeus had to get beyond what other people said. So do you!

What you and I have to realize is that the vast majority of people making up the human race are negative, doom and gloom, naysayers.

You see, since most people who attempt to climb out of a rut end up climbing back in, people around get to believing that is the norm. That is what to expect. Most of them aren't willing to risk encouraging someone who won't be daunted by those odds. They might get laughed at for making rash predictions. So they take the safe route. They conclude that you won't make it. They will even try to talk you out of trying to get out of the rut and try to discourage you.

That's why the Bible warns us about the company we keep. If we hang around and listen to fearful or negative people, we'll become fearful and negative. I find it interesting that in certain key battles in the Old Testament, God sent those who were fearful home, even though it lessened the number of troops.

We have to stop worrying about what other people will say. What they say often has no basis in concern for you. They're only saying what they think is the safest thing to say. So if you listen to the crowd, you'll stay in the rut. Guaranteed! Stop worrying about what other people will say!

5) Stop Waiting For Ideal Circumstances

The situation on the day Bartimaeus was healed was far from ideal. Verse 46 says that Jesus was going out from Jericho with His disciples and a great multitude. What chance did anyone have of getting Jesus' attention in such a large crowd? Hardly any. So what chance did a blind man have?

Perhaps, Bartimaeus should have waited for a better time. Maybe tomorrow or the next day or next week or next year circumstances will be better.

That's classic rut dweller language, isn't it?

Waiting for ideal circumstances will leave you in a rut-a rut that could ultimately become a grave. Stop waiting for ideal circumstances.

6) Take A Bold Step Of Faith

Verse 50 says, "*And casting aside his cloak, he jumped up, and came to Jesus.*" Hey, we're talking about risk here, aren't we? It's scary! Probably some of you have already dismissed me and decided to keep to the security of your rut. That's certainly you're choice. But at least be honest about it. Quit blaming others.

Bartimaeus put it all out front for everyone to see. What a big, bold, open, public stand to take. He wanted out of his rut!

Are you willing to do something bold? Are you willing to take a stand in front of others? "I don't think something that drastic is necessary," you say. Maybe not, but have your less drastic measures worked for you? Maybe it's time to get bold! Do something bold and dramatic.

7) Make Your Move Now

Most people never get out of the rut because they never make a move in that direction. They always find an excuse not to make a move even though they know that a move is the best thing for them.

Bartimaeus had no idea Jesus was coming to his town that day. This day was just like every other to him as he climbed off his sleeping pallet and felt his way down to his familiar spot beside the road. He didn't have time to prepare. It was suddenly just there.

I'm not suggesting that you shouldn't take time to plan. But do something now or this occasion will become just like all the others where you didn't break out of your grave. Make your move now!

WRITTEN IN STONE

The Best is Yet to Come
Francis Albert Sinatra
located in Desert Memorial Park, Cathedral City, California

FINAL WORDS

I hope I haven't bored you.
(Concluding what would be his last press conference.)
--Elvis Presley, died 1977

CHAPTER 19
Dead Ringer

"For death is no more than a turning of us over from time to eternity."
-William Penn

I remember as a youngster of having nightmares of being "buried alive." I think it was because of an old Alfred Hitchcock Mystery Presents television episode that was surrounded by this frightening concept. Today's society calls it "taphophobia," which literally means the fear of graves. The extreme fear of being buried alive was so evident in ages past that those that were wealthy enough had special devices built-in their caskets that would ensure this could never happen. They had special air pipes installed on their caskets or strings to an outside bell in the cemetery that could be pulled from the inside letting the outside world know that they were still alive.

According to urban legends that's where we get the phrases "saved by the bell" and "dead ringer."

In the Christian walk, we sometimes experience an "entrapment" that can be as frightening as my nightmares of the casket lid closing on me months before my eyes ever decide to. This death in the individual Christian or sometimes the entire church body is called legalism. The long-term effect can be absolutely devastating if we allow the lid to stay shut.

You may say that legalism isn't a problem in today's society. Let's go to the extreme first and then take a few steps back to see the disease in the right perspective. For instance, almost every state in our nation still has laws on their books that would surprise most people. For example,

In Alabama:

*It is illegal to play Dominos on Sunday.

*It is illegal to wear a fake moustache that causes laughter in church.

*Putting salt on a railroad track may be punishable by death.

In Alaska:

*In Fairbanks, it is illegal to feed alcoholic beverages to a moose.

*While it is legal to shoot bears, waking sleeping bears for the purpose of taking a photograph is prohibited.

In California:

*In Los Angeles, a man may legally beat his wife with a leather strap, as long as it is less than two inches wide, or she gives him permission to use a wider strap.

*It is a misdemeanor to shoot at any kind of game from a moving vehicle, unless the target is a whale.

In West Virginia:

*In Nicholas County, no clergy members may tell jokes or humorous stories from the pulpit during church services.

*Doctors and dentists may not place a woman under anesthesia unless a third person is present.

*It is illegal to snooze on a train.

These silly laws may make us laugh because they seem so absurd and ridiculous. But, it we were to list all the rules, expectations, and laws that are "on the books" in many churches today, chances are we'd stop laughing pretty quickly. Most of these religious regulations are not written down anywhere but many of us either attempt to keep them, or expect others to do so.

Before we get too deep in our discussion let's briefly look at some scripture. Colossians 2:14 says, *"God forgave us all our sins, having canceled the written code, with its regulations, that was against us and that stood opposed to us; he took it away, nailing it to the cross."* Then move on down to Colossians 2:20-23: *"Since you died with Christ to the basic principles of this world, why, as though you still belonged to it, do you submit to its rules: 'Do not handle! Do not taste! Do not touch!?' Therese are all destined to perish with use, because they are based on human commands and teachings, their false humility and their harsh treatment of the body, but they lack any value in retraining sensual indulgence."*

The grave danger of legalism is that it reduces the Christian life to a set of rules and regulations, and when a legalist keeps the rules, he feels good about himself. But in reality growth can be stunted, or even choked to death by the weeds of legalism.

Legalism can be defined as a strict adherence to the law. Specifically, as it relates to faith, a legalist is one who believes that performance is the way to gain favor with God. Legalism is the human attempt to gain salvation or prove our spiritually by outward conformity to a list of religious "do's and don'ts." Beware it is often disguised in Christian terms and behavior.

A few warnings about legalism:

1) We usually tend to think others are legalistic, but that we're not. Imagine that! The fact is that we're all legalistic by nature. We tend to judge others by our own standards of what is acceptable and what isn't. In essence, we think our sins smell better than other people's. We seem to have very little tolerance for people who sin differently that we do.

2) Legalism is highly contagious. While it's usually less conscious in our minds than is was among the Pharisees, legalism can spread like a bad virus through an entire congregation. That's why Jesus reserved some of his harshest criticism for legalistic list-makers in Mark 7:6-8: *"These people honor me with their lips, but their hearts are far from me. They worship me in vain; their teachings are but rules taught by men."*

3) Legalism can take a vibrant and alive faith and make it dull and full of death quickly. It can evaporate enthusiasm and stifle spirituality. Instead of finding freedom through Christ, many believers become burdened by the church. Ouch!

4) Legalism produces large quantities of self-righteousness, judgment and condemnation. It majors in guilt and misguided sacrifice, urging its followers to evaluate their relationship with God on the basis of standards and scores and expects others to do the same. Superficial spiritually short-circuits the work of grace.

5) Legalism makes us narrow-minded and divisive. The legalist insists that everyone live up to the standard they have adopted. In other words, everyone needs to be like me. When we think this way, we miss the delight of diversity in the church.

6) Legalism makes it impossible for people to see Jesus. There is nothing that pushes a seeker away faster than a list of rules and regulations. We inadvertently portray Jesus as a drill sergeant instead of the Savior.

This "death trap" was starting to take over in the church at Colosse. They were needed a quick and important lesson on grace. We're saved by grace and we grow by grace. Anything else is done in vain. Paul in Colossians 2:9-15 argues that if we don't want death in our Christian walk we must remember our legal standing with the Lord.

What do I mean by legal standing with the Lord? If we understand God's divine decree as a result of what Jesus has done on our behalf, we'll experience amazing grace and live with the freedom that is ours in Christ. Listen to what Jesus said in John 8:36, *"So if the Son sets you free, you will be free indeed."*

When we accept Jesus as our Lord and Savior God issues four rulings or decrees.

*We are complete. See what Colossians 2:9-11 says, *"For in Christ all the fullness of the Deity lives in bodily form, and you have been given fullness in Christ, who is the head over every power and authority."* The phrase, "in Christ" shows us that Jesus is the center of God's saving activity. When we put our faith in Christ, we are included in what He has done. All the fullness of deity lives in Him. Jesus is not just a way to God; He is the only way because He is God Himself.

You have everything you need if you have Christ because the fullness of God comes into your life when you receive Jesus. Listen, you do not need anything more than you already have! You merely need to understand and appropriate that which you've already been given.

*We are alive. Colossians 2:11-13a says, *"In Him you were also circumcised, in the putting off of the sinful nature, not with a circumcision done by the hands of men but with the circumcision done by Christ, having been buried with Him baptism and raised with Him through your faith in the power of God, who raised Him from the dead. When you were dead in your sins and in the uncircumcision of your sinful nature, God made you alive with Christ."*

God initiated the circumcision in the Old Testament as part of His covenant with His people in order to set them apart and identify them as true followers. One of the problems at Colosse was that some legalists were demanding that Christians submit to circumcision and obey the Old Testament Law. There false teachers were a bit different than those Paul refuted in Galatians. In that context, they were insisting that circumcision was necessary for salvation. In the church at Colosse, the false teachers were suggesting that obedience to Old Testament regulations would help them become more spiritual.

When we put our faith in Christ, Jesus spiritually circumcises, or cuts away, our sinful nature in order to prove that we belong to Him. Since we are alive, and no longer dead in our sins, Paul next uses the illustration of baptism. The word baptize has both a literal and figurative meaning. The literal meaning is "to dip, or immerse." The figurative meaning is "to be identified with."

Remembering that our old sinful nature is dead and buried with Christ gives us a powerful motive to resist sin. We can keep sinful desires from controlling us by treating them as if they are dead. Romans 6:11-14 provides a practical game plan to use in order to live with the freedom that Christ has promised us: *"In the same way, count yourselves dead to sin but alive to God in Christ Jesus. Therefore do not let sin reign in your mortal body so that you obey its evil desires. Do not offer the parts of your body to sin, as instruments of wickedness, but rather offer yourselves to God, as those who have been brought from death to life; and offer the parts of your body to him as instruments of righteousness. For sin shall not be your master, because you are not under law, but under grace."*

*Our sins are canceled. Colossians 2:13a-14 continues on with, *"He forgave us all our sins, having canceled the written code, with its regulations, that was against us and that stood opposed to us; He took it away, nailing it to the cross."*

Here we see that we're not only complete and alive, but our sins have been canceled. Notice that Jesus forgave "all" our sins. That means every single one, even those that you have a hard time forgiving yourself for. The "written code" is the Law. Jesus not only took our sins to the cross, He also took the Law and nailed it there, forever. The Law was against us and stood opposed to us because all it could ever do was point out our sinfulness. In Romans 7:7, Paul concludes that he *"would not have known what sin was except through the law."*

*We have victory. Colossians 2:15 says *"And having disarmed the powers and authorities, He made a public spectacle of them, triumphing over them by the cross."* We now have completeness in Christ, we have new life, and we have been completely forgiven!

The powers and authorities of this evil world stripped Christ of His clothing and popularity, made a public spectacle of Him on the cross, and thought they had triumphed over Him by putting Him to death. Little did they know that the victory actually belonged to Jesus. Evil no longer has any power over you because Christ has stripped Satan's weapons from him. He is disarmed. The only power he has is what we give him when we allow him to deceive us and create fear in our lives.

1 Corinthians 15:54-57 sums up our position when it declares, *"Death has been swallowed up in victory. Where, O death, is your victory? Where, O death, is your sting? The sting of death is sin, and the power of sin is the law. But thanks be to God! He gives us the victory through our Lord Jesus Christ."*

WRITTEN IN STONE

A Gentle Man and a Gentleman
Jack Dempsey
located in Southampton Cemetery; Southampton, New York

FINAL WORDS

Cool it, brothers...
(His last words before being assassinated.)
Malcolm X, died 1965

CHAPTER 20
All Dressed Up and No Place to Go

"A time to be born and a time to die."
-Ecclesiastes 3:2

GRAVE CLOTHES. Definition: The clothes or dress in which the dead are interred.

An old one-line joke that has been floating around for years is the engraving found on an atheist's tombstone: "Here lies an atheist; all dressed up and no place to go." Of course, we know that there are only two places that are available to attend after death, no matter how you are dressed.

The Word of God uses several metaphors to describe the Christian life. A common metaphor is the picture of taking off old clothes and putting on new clothes when you become a born again believer. That's the exact picture that we find in Colossians 3. But be careful that you don't take this analogy literally. Clothes are simply external coverings and the Christian life is concerned more with internal change than in external coverings. We as believers must shift gears in our approach to Christianity and start being more concerned with the internal condition of our relationship with Christ and not so obsessed with the external clothing.

As we continue our journey through the book of Colossians, we notice that the first two chapters of Colossians teach us what to believe, and now the last two chapters teach us how to behave.

Colossians 3:5-12. *"Put to death, therefore, whatever belongs to your earthly nature: sexual immorality, impurity, lust, evil desires and greed, which is idolatry. Because of these, the wrath of God is coming. You used to walk in these ways, in the life you once lived. But now you must rid yourselves of all such things as these: anger, rage, malice, slander, and filthy language from your lips. Do not lie to each other, since you have taken off your old self with its practices and have put on the new self, which is being renewed in knowledge in the image of its Creator. Here there is no Greek or Jew, circumcised or uncircumcised, barbarian, Scythian, slave or free, but Christ is all, and is in all. Therefore, as God's chosen people, holy and dearly loved, clothe yourselves with compassion, kindness, humility, gentleness and patience."*

One of my favorite miracles that Jesus performed is the raising of His best friend, Lazarus. You have probably heard dozens of sermons and studied tons of Bible lessons on Lazarus, but every time a new nugget of truth is revealed. The fascinating truth about scripture is that every miracle of Jesus contains a parable and every parable of Jesus contains a miracle. In John 11, Jesus performs a miracle illustrating this spiritual truth of taking off the old clothes and putting on the new.

You know the story, but let's revisit it again and search for another truth. Martha and Mary, the sisters of Lazarus, sent word for Jesus to come back home because Lazarus was sick. Jesus delayed His return home for several days, and during the delay Lazarus died. The disciples were confused by this, and when Jesus finally arrived in Bethany, both sisters said to Him, "Master if you had been here my brother wouldn't have died." When Jesus saw their grief, and the grief of others who loved Lazarus, the Bible says Jesus wept with them.

With his eyes filled with tears, Jesus approached Lazarus' tomb and gave instructions for the stone to be removed. Martha objected saying, "Lord, by this time there is a bad odor, for he has been dead four days." I just love the way the KJV puts it, "He stinketh." That's probably the understatement of the world. But anyway, Jesus said, "Did I not tell you if you believed you would see the glory of God?" They rolled the stone away and Jesus spoke in a voice loud enough to raise the dead: "LAZARUS, COME FORTH!" I remember hearing a preacher say once it's a good thing Jesus specified Lazarus by name, or else every corpse in the graveyard would have come back to life!

At the sound of Jesus' summons, Lazarus came stumbling and hopping out of the tomb. In those days, corpses were wrapped in long pieces of cloth soaked in spices. When Lazarus came out of the tomb, he was still wrapped in those stinking grave clothes. He couldn't talk, and he couldn't walk. He had received life, but he still had a problem—those pesky grave clothes!

That's the story I want to use to introduce this final chapter. Lazarus had been given life when he was dead–that's a picture of salvation. But he was still bound by those old stinking grave clothes. Many Christians today face the same problem. Jesus gives us life, but we still struggle with the stinking grave clothes of our old life.

In some ways, we're like Lazarus. He was saved, but he still stunk. He was rescued but he was still reeking. He was energized, but he was still entrapped. He had life, but he wasn't liberated. When we compare this story about Lazarus with our text in Colossians, we discover the importance of getting rid of those old stinking grave clothes.

The raising of Lazarus from the dead is most striking portrayal of what occurs when one who is lost and dead in sin is given life everlasting through faith in Christ. We are told that when Jesus cried with a loud voice, *"Lazarus, come forth,"* he who was dead emerged from the tomb *"bound hand and foot with grave clothes; and his face was bound about with a napkin"* (John 11:44). Here was a wonderful miracle, and yet he who was raised had his hands and feet bound like a mummy, and his face wrapped about with a cloth. What a picture of many who indeed have been brought to life through faith in Christ, but who still are not fit for service because of certain hindering remnants of the old life that must first be removed.

Did you catch that? There's that nugget of truth I was talking about. Are you ready?

*His mouth.

Notice that Lazarus' face was bound, implying that his mouth was covered. This is symbolic of those who, although spiritually alive, still have their mouths gagged by the "grave clothes" of worldly habits. In many ways they may be eloquent in their speech, but in the spiritual things they are silent. They can pray a prayer that sounds so grand with all the "thees and thous" flowing from it, but then still cuss like a sailor outside of the church walls.

I hear it all the time, Greg, relax, chill out and loosen up. Thanks but no thanks. Our conversation and the words we use should reflect the love we have for Christ. It hampers our relationship with the Lord and causes the world to stumble when we use the "filthy language" in our daily conversations.

Here is a great test. Next time you want to know if the person you are talking to has a deep relationship with the Lord, just "hush" for a few moments and listen to them. What words are they using? Either the words of this world will gush from their lips or the Living Word will flow from their hearts. There is no mistake in this. It will be so evident. Just listen.

*His hands and feet were bound.

Lazarus' hands and feet were bound. This is a metaphor that speaks of restricted service. Many Christians do very little or nothing for the Lord because they are still "bound" by their selfish attitudes and the distracting cares of this life. Not only are they hampered in their Christian walk by those things which characterized their *"former conversation"* but they are powerless because of the limited use of their service for Jesus. It is so important to get rid of these bindings of the world with their *"deceitful lusts"* (Ephesians 4:22).

Removing the grave clothes means taking off the old things of this world that hinders the spiritual power such as *"anger, wrath, malice, blasphemy, (and) filthy communication out of (out) mouth"* (Colossians 3:8). Only after we have *"put off... the old man"* of sin and carnality will we be ready to *"meet for the Master's use"* (2 Timothy 2:21).

So what are we suppose according to do with these verses?

1) Throw away the old grave clothes.

Verse 10 tells us *"since you have taken off your old self"* indicates to us that we are delivered from the penalty of sin, but also implies that the presence of sin is still a reality in our lives. This section of scripture is written so believers can have some comfort when they are still struggling with their old habits. Paul even described his own battle in his personal life when he penned in Romans 7, *"I find myself doing the things I don't want to do. And I have a desire to do the right things, but sometimes I don't."* Paul continues with a great question, *"Who shall release me from this body of death?"*

Then Paul answers his very own question with another nugget of truth. Jesus Christ is the only reliable source of strength to overcome this old life and bring the fullness of the new life into action.

Paul tells us in Colossians 3:5 to *"Put to death, therefore, whatever belongs to your earthly nature: sexual immorality, impurity, lust, evil desires and greed, which is idolatry."* That's the old life, the old clothes, the old things. Get rid of them. They can't continue to dwell in the life of a Christian without affecting your relationship with the Master.

After that list of sins, you may be feeling pretty confident that you have conquered those giants in your life and you're feeling pretty self-assured that you are "squeaky clean." But then the scripture continues on and declares in Colossians 3:8, *"Rid yourselves of all such things as these: anger, rage, malice, slander, and filthy language from your lips. Do not lie to each other."*

Ouch! Most of can handle the first list, but the second list grabs us and can pull us down into the trenches if we are not careful. This list of sins basically has to do with what we say or how we say something. Christians are quick to judge others regarding the first list of sins, but quickly backtrack on this second list of violations. They both are equally destructive to our walk, to our testimony and to our witness to others. The Bible tells us to discard of all the old practices and become new in the Lord.

2) Put on your new clothes.

The Bible clearly states that we should throw away the old clothes and put on the new. Think about it, if you were out fishing all day and getting sweaty and stinky from all the fish guts and worm juice and then you wanted to take your wife out to eat for a nice romantic dinner. You wouldn't just come home from the lake and put the clean, fresh clothes over the smelly and stinking clothes would you? Or try to cover the smell with a quick spray of "Old Spice?"

So let's continue this little story. The dinner goes fine and as the evening progresses the dance music begins and you take your wife's hand and proceed to the dance floor. Picture it? You put your loving arms around your wife's waist and pull her close to your chest as the soft, slow music begins. You look into her eyes with great passion and you start to dance. But then you notice your wife starts to wiggle her nose and under her breath mentions that something smells "fishy."

No matter how hard you tried to cover the earlier activities of the day, I guarantee that before the evening's event was finished, your wife would have a few things to say about it.

The Bible says that the Christian life is like putting on a new, clean set of clothes. New. Brand spanking new. The problem arises when we just want to put the new over the old and pretend we smell ok. But when we start to dance with the Lord, He will smell the old, filthy life penetrating through. It will affect the relationship. He demands a new life, a new walk, a new direction. He is worthy of this.

Don't cover the old life up. Get rid of it and put on the new clothes of Jesus Christ.

Let's find one more nugget of truth before we close this chapter down. Let's go back to the story of Lazarus and his grave clothes. John 11:44 says, *"The dead man came out, his hands and feet wrapped with strips of linen, and a cloth around his face. Jesus said to them, "Take off the grave clothes and let him go."*

Let's go back to our story of Lazarus and those stinking grave clothes. I've studied this story for years and even preached on it many times. But there is a powerful truth in this story I never noticed before. This week as I was praying over this message, the Lord gave me a new insight into a truth I had missed all these years. The Bible says in John 11:44: *"The dead man came out, his hands and feet wrapped with strips of linen, and a cloth around his face. Jesus said to them, "Take off the grave clothes and let him go."*

Two commandments were declared by the Lord that day. First, "Lazarus, Come forth!"

Second, "Take off the grave clothes and let him go!" This second command is a perfect illustration to the church. We need to help each other out of their grave clothes. Jesus could have just simply said the word and Lazarus' grave clothes would have disappeared miraculously. But Jesus wanted to get the other people involved in the ministry. He wanted them to feel the excitement of unwrapping a once "deader than a doornail" corpse.

The church should be exactly the same way. We shouldn't expect everyone to clean up their own life by themselves. We need to help them out of their old grave clothes. One piece at a time. One strip at a time. The Bible says, *"Brothers, if someone is caught up in a sin, you who are spiritual should restore him gently. Carry each other's burdens, and in this way you will fulfill the law of Christ."* (Galatians 6:1-2)

Watch this. Jesus told those standing around to remove the grave clothes that had Lazarus bound. Can you just image the fun and excitement unwrapping Lazarus was! With each strip of cloth removed, more of his body became free! What a party that must have started right there in the middle of the cemetery!

Are you sick and tired of the old life? Are you ready to receive the new life? Are you ready to be free? Make a phone call to the undertaker and tell him that you're not ready for him yet. Then pull yourself out of that grave, jump out of that casket and start striping off those old, stinky grave clothes and experience the fullness of a new life that can only be found in Jesus. Do it now. Do it today. Before it's too late!

WRITTEN IN STONE

Here was buried Thomas Jefferson,
author of the Declaration of American Independence,
of the statute of Virginia for religious freedom,
and father of the University of Virginia.
Thomas Jefferson
located in Monticello, Virginia

FINAL WORDS

If someone is going to kill me, they will kill me.
(On arriving in Dallas, 1963)
John F. Kennedy, died 1963

CHAPTER 21
Dead End

"When the game is over,
the king and the pawn go into the same box."
-Italian Proverb

REFLECTION AND REVIEW DAY:

If you haven't figured it out by now....please get some help. This is the time of the week that you should find some time in your schedule. Alone time. Private time. Quiet time. Just you, your thoughts, and your Creator, Jesus. Grab your Bible and sneak away. Go ahead....it's not a sin. Apply the truth. Soak in the Spirit. Open your heart and let the Word fill it completely. It will feel so good, I promise. Ready..... go for it.

Chapter 15: Dead Man Walking"

*Have you experience a "major" life-changing event in your life? What was it? How did it affect the direction of your life?

*Write out the details of that event. How you ever used that eye-opening chapter in your life to witness and testify to someone else. If not, why?

*How would you describe your Christian walk....alive or dead?

Chapter 16: Dead Man Walking, Part 2"

*What is your personal view of who you are IN Christ?

*What are your expectations of your life through Christ? Are you reaching your ultimate potential through Jesus or just existing?

*Identify two or three people that are in your life right now that needs that extra encouragement to become everything that God wants them to be. Are you willing to lending a hand in that encouragement?

Chapter 17: Dead Poets Society"

*Reread Colossians 1:9-12. What do these verses mean to you?

____

____

____

____

*What do you feel is God's specific purpose for your life? Are you living out that purpose right now?

____

____

____

____

*What elements of the fruit of the Spirit found in Galatians 5:22-23 do you possess in your life? Which ones still need some work?

____

____

____

____

*What's your definition of true success in a Christian's life?

____

____

____

____

Chapter 18: The Final Interment?

*Evaluate your Christian walk right now. What "ruts" are you currently in that needs to be redirected?

____

____

____

____

*Is there an area in your life that you have blamed on someone else when in reality you haven't taken the personal responsibility for that action?

____

____

____

____

*Spend a few moments right now specifying areas in your walk that need to be clarified. Do you have the faith that life can soon flow from this area in your life?

____

____

____

____

*Are you ready to make that life-changing decision now?

____

____

____

____

Chapter 19: Dead Ringer"

*What traces of legalism exists in your attitudes and judgments on others?

____

____

____

____

*Where do you think that these thoughts came from?

____

____

____

____

*Have you accepted the four decrees from Christ including:

1) We are complete in Christ
2) We are alive in Christ
3) Our sins are canceled by Christ
4) We have victory through Christ

Chapter 20: "All Dressed Up and No Place to Go"

*What part of the "old life" are you still wearing?

*What area of your life needs to be loosened and given over to the Lord?

-your mouth?

-your hands?

-your eyes?

*Do you know of someone that needs help getting out of their "old grave clothes"?

*How can you help them put on the new Christ?

WRITTEN IN STONE

Tomorrow is the most important thing in life.
Comes into us at midnight very clean.
It's perfect when it arrives and it puts itself in our hands.
It hopes we've learned something from yesterday.
John Wayne
Located in Pacific View Memorial Park
Cemetery, Corona del Mar, California

FINAL WORDS

I'm going away tonight.
(Reported by his personal manager, Charles Bobbit,
who said he was at Brown's bedside when he died,
and added that Brown said the statement above, then
took three long, quiet breaths, and closed his eyes.)
--James Brown, died 2006

EPILOGUE

'Spit the Grave Dust Out of Your Mouth and Live!'

"Death is more universal than life; everyone dies but not everyone lives."
-A. Sachs

While I was putting the final touches on this book, I realized that I need to conclude the work with an Epilogue. Then I asked myself, "What's an Epilogue?" So I went to the internet for my quick answer and typed in "epilogue" and this is what I found: Epilogue; a closing section added to a literary work, providing further comment, interpretation, or information, a conclusion. Oh, that's what an epilogue is!

Well, I'm not in complete agreement with the definition of an epilogue because this is not the ending of the book. This is only the beginning. One of my favorite Christian music artist is David Phelps, formally of the New Gaither Vocal Band, has a fantastic song entitled, "The End of the Beginning." That is what my wish and prayer for you is. Don't just finish the book and lay it down and never think about anything that you've read. Put the book into action. Activate the principals and design a direction and formulate a plan of action for you and your family right now. Remember this isn't the end; it's just the end of the beginning for you. Now is your opportunity to change.

Change. Ouch! Just saying that word hurts sometimes. We get in a rut (which we've already discussed earlier in the book) and routine that has created a false sense of security, because sometimes the direction we are headed is cemetery bound instead of life with the Lord.

Change. Here are a few wonderful thoughts on change to motivate you to think in that direction. Benjamin Franklin is given credit for both of these tidbits of wisdom. "Life is change. Growth is optional. Choose wisely." Here's the other one, "When you're finished changing, you're finished." Reread the quotes again. Are you willing to make the effort to change, to grow, to develop into all that the Lord has in store for you?

Now listen to what Jesus said about change in Matthew 18:1-4: "At that time the disciples came to Jesus and asked, 'Who is the greatest in the kingdom of heaven?' He called a little child and had him stand among them. And He said, 'I tell you the truth, unless you **CHANGE** and become like little children, you will never enter the kingdom of heaven. Therefore, whoever humbles himself like this child is the greatest in the kingdom of heaven."

Do you think it was an accident that Jesus deliberately used a child as an example? Nah. He loved the passion children have for life. He enjoyed being in their presence, because they are so full of LIFE. Ever been around a whole group of older "saints"? They start to outline all of their pains, hurts and agonies from their backaches to their bunions and then finish off with their latest experience in the bathroom. That's not life, that's misery! The Lord used children as the example because they love life and lift up the excitement of living with the anticipation of the next adventure that awaits them just around the corner.

Kids love to have fun. They see so much wonder in the world around them. Look at the face of a child when they see a puppy or when they play in the mud after a summer rain shower. They squeeze every ounce out of life each and every day. It's about time that we change and become more like these children in our lives.

Are you ready to walk through that door into the "great unknown" called change? First of all, I must take care of first things first. Have you experienced salvation? Have you asked Jesus Christ to be your Lord and Savior? Today is the day. Now is the time. Change. The ultimate change from death into life. If you follow the ABCs and sincerely desire for the Lord to enter into your heart, it will happen. A: Admit that you have sinned. B: Believe in Jesus and ask Him to enter into your heart. C: Confess your sins and call on Jesus to save your soul from death and let's go ahead and throw in D: Decide to do it now. Now pray this prayer, "Jesus, I believe you died for me and rose from the dead, so now I want to live for You. I am turning away from my sins and placing my trust in You. I acknowledge You as my Savior and Lord, and I'm asking You to guide my life from now on. Amen."

If you said that with heartfelt belief then your life has been changed for all eternity. Please let me know by e-mailing me at bodybagreligion@yahoo.com I want to share in your decision and excitement. Praise the Lord!

If you are already a Christian then maybe this book will help you to "come alive." Remember the children. I would like to close with this writing from an Anonymous source, but it is so true with our daily lives. It goes like this:

"I am hereby officially tendering my resignation as an adult. I have decided I would like to accept the responsibilities of an 8-year-old again. I want to go to McDonald's and think that it's a four-star restaurant. I want to think M&Ms are better than money because you can eat them. I want to return to a time when life was simple. When all you knew were colors, multiplications tables, and nursery rhymes, but that didn't bother you, because you didn't know what you didn't know and you didn't care. All you knew was to be happy because you were blissfully unaware of all the things that should make you worried or upset. I want to think the world is fair. That everyone is honest and good. I want to believe that anything is possible. I want to be oblivious to the complexities of life and be overly excited again. I don't want my day to consist of computer crashes, mountains of paperwork, depressing news, doctor bills, and gossip. I want to believe in the power of smiles, hugs, a kind word, truth, justice, peace, dreams, imagination, mankind, and making angels in the snow. So…Here's my checkbook and my car keys, my credit card bills and my 401K statements. I am officially resigning from adulthood. And if you want to discuss this further, you'll have to catch me first, 'cause…. "Tag! You're it!"

Isn't that wonderful? Now's the time. Open up the casket, crawl out of the grave, get rid of the grave clothes, throw the body bag away, spit the grave dirt out of your mouth and start to live. Start to dance, because the music of this life doesn't last forever. Start living today before it's too late.

THE END? You decide!

Printed in the United States
116691LV00004B/49-168/P

9 781434 390240